Come, Thou

Long-Expected

Jesus

Come, Thou Long-Expected Jesus

EXPERIENCING THE PEACE AND PROMISE OF CHRISTMAS

EDITED BY

Nancy Guthrie

WHEATON, ILLINOIS

Cover Image and Design: Jordan Singer
First printing 2008
Reprinted with new cover 2020
Printed in China

Chapter 2 Scripture quotations are from *The New American Standard Bible®*. Copyright © 1960, 1962, 1963, 1968, 1971, 1972, 1973, 1975, 1977 , 1995 by The Lockman Foundation. Used by permission. www.Lockman.org.

Chapters 3, 6, 8, 9, and 17 Scripture quotations are from the King James Version of the Bible. Public domain.

Chapter opening quotations and chapters 4, 13, and 20 Scripture quotations are from the ESV® Bible (The Holy Bible, English Standard Version®), copyright © 2001 by Crossway, a publishing ministry of Good News Publishers. Used by permission. All rights reserved.

Chapters 5, 11, 14, 16, 18, 19, 21, and 22 Scripture quotations are taken from the Holy Bible: New International Version®. NIV®. Copyright © 1973, 1978, 1984 by International Bible Society. Used by permission of Zondervan. All rights reserved worldwide.

Chapter 15 Scripture references are from The New King James Version®. Copyright © 1982 by Thomas Nelson. Used by permission. All rights reserved.

Scripture references marked PHILLIPS are from The New Testament in Modern English by J. B. Phillips © 1960, 1972 J. B. Phillips. Administered by The Archbishops' Council of the Church of England. Used by permission.

All emphases in Scripture quotations have been added by the authors.

Hardcover ISBN: 978-1-4335-7311-8

Library of Congress Cataloging-in-Publication Data

Come, thou long expected Jesus : experiencing the peace and promise of Christmas / edited by Nancy Guthrie.
　　　　p. cm.
Includes bibliographical references.
　　ISBN 978-1-4335-0180-7 (tpb)
　　1. Christmas—Meditations. 2. Christmas sermons. I. Guthrie, Nancy. II. Title.
BV45.C595　　　　　2008
242'.335—dc22　　　　　　　　　　　　　　　　　　　　2008013262

Crossway is a publishing ministry of Good News Publishers.

RRDS		32	31	30	29	28	27	26	25	24	23	22
15	14	13	12	11	10	9	8	7	6	5	4	3

Affectionately dedicated to
Dr. Wilson and Pam Benton
who incarnated the love of God
by making your home among us—
full of grace and truth

O God, take me in spirit to the watchful shepherds,
and enlarge my mind;
Let me hear good tidings of great joy, and hearing,
believe, rejoice, praise, adore,
my conscience bathed in an ocean of repose, my
eyes uplifted to a reconciled Father;
place me with ox, ass, camel, goat, to look with
them upon my Redeemer's face, and in him
account myself delivered from sin;
let me with Simeon clasp the new-born child to my
heart,
embrace him with undying faith,
exulting that he is mine and I am his.
In him thou has given me so much that heaven can
give no more.

—from *The Valley of Vision*

Contents

Preface

My husband tells the story of a Christmas when his family had to wait to open their Christmas gifts while he went into his bedroom to wrap the gifts he had bought. "What's the matter, David?" his grandmother asked as he emerged from his room with his stack of hastily wrapped presents. "Did Christmas sneak up on you this year?"

I have found in my own life that I've too often allowed Christmas to "sneak up on me." I've allowed the busyness of purchasing presents and planning travel and participating in Christmas pageants and parties to crowd out a quiet anticipation of the wonder of incarnation. Too many Christmas mornings I've realized that while my presents were wrapped, my heart was completely unprepared to truly take in the Gift.

A while back a friend recommended a particular anthology of readings for Advent. So early in December when I saw a large display of the books in a bookstore, I purchased a copy and began to read.

While some of the readings were interesting and inspiring, some left me cold, and others left me confused. But when I came to one particular reading, I just set the book aside. In a piece discussing differences in the accounts of the birth of Jesus, the writer suggested that Scripture doesn't have to be historical to be inspired.

I began to think about how much I would enjoy a similar book with short readings on Advent themes from a number of different writers I trust and respect; that reflected a high view of Scripture; and that put the incarnation in the context of God's unfolding plan of redemption. And not finding such a book available, I embarked on what has been a sacred adventure of putting such a collection together.

What a profound blessing it has been to read through written works and listen to sermons of some of the best theologians and Bible teachers of all time, searching for treasures of insight on the familiar Christmas story. I've edited excerpts from writings and sermons into meditations that I pray will illumine your mind, awaken your longing, and prepare your heart for a fresh experience of the coming of Jesus this season.

Nancy Guthrie

1

Contemplating Christmas

GEORGE WHITEFIELD

"But Mary treasured up all these things, pondering them in her heart."

Luke 2:19

I t was love, mere love; it was free love that brought the Lord Jesus Christ into our world. What, shall we not remember the birth of our Jesus? Shall we yearly celebrate the birth of our temporal king, and shall that of the King of kings be quite forgotten? Shall that only, which ought to be had chiefly in remembrance, be quite forgotten? God forbid! No, my dear brethren, let us celebrate and keep this festival of our church with joy in our hearts: let the birth of a Redeemer, which redeemed us from sin, from wrath, from death, from hell, be always remembered; may this Savior's love never be forgotten! But may we sing forth all his love and glory as long as life shall last here, and through an endless eternity in the world above! May we chant forth the wonders of redeeming love and the riches of free grace, amidst angels and archangels, cherubim and seraphim, without intermission, forever and ever! And as, my brethren, the time for keeping this festival is approaching, let us consider our duty in the true observation thereof, of the right way for the glory of God, and the good of immortal souls, to celebrate the birth of our Lord Jesus Christ; an event which ought to be had in eternal remembrance.

What can we do to employ our time to a more noble purpose than reading of what our dear Redeemer has done and suffered; to read that the King of kings and the Lord of lords came from his throne and took upon him the form of the meanest of his servants; and what great things he underwent. This, this is a history worth reading, this is worth employing our time about: and surely, when we read of the sufferings of our Savior, it should excite us to prayer, that we might have an interest in the Lord Jesus Christ; that the blood which he spilt upon Mount Calvary, and his death and crucifixion, might make an atonement for our sins, that we might be made holy; that we might be enabled to put off the old man with his deeds, and put on the new man, even the Lord Jesus Christ; that we may throw away the heavy yoke of sin, and put on the yoke of the Lord Jesus Christ.

Let us consider our duty in the true observation thereof, of the right way for the glory of God, and the good of immortal souls, to celebrate the birth of our Lord Jesus Christ.

Indeed, my brethren, these things call for prayer, and for earnest prayer too; and O do be earnest with God, that you may have an interest in this Redeemer, and that you may put on his righteousness, so that you may not come before him in your filthy rags, nor be found not having on the wedding garment. O do not, I beseech you, trust unto yourselves for justification; you cannot, indeed, you cannot be justified by the works of the law. I entreat that your time may be thus spent; and if you are in company, let your time be spent in that conversation which prof-iteth: let it not be about your dressing, your plays, your profits, or your worldly concerns, but let it be the wonders of redeeming love. O tell, tell to each other what great things the Lord has done for your souls; declare unto one another how you were delivered from the hands of your common enemy, Satan, and how the Lord has brought your feet from the clay and has set them upon the rock of ages, the Lord Jesus Christ; there, my brethren, is no slipping. Other conversation, by often repeating, you become fully acquainted with, but of Christ there is always something new to raise your thoughts; you can never want when the love of the Lord Jesus Christ is the subject. So let Jesus be the subject, my brethren, of all your conversation.

Did Jesus come into the world to save us from death, and shall we spend no part of our time in conversing about our dear Jesus?

Let your time be spent on him: O this, this is an employ, which if you belong to Jesus, will last you to all eternity.

Let me beseech you to have a regard, a particular regard to your behavior, at this time; for indeed the eyes of all are upon you, and they would rejoice much to find any reason to complain of you. They can say things against us without a cause; and how would they rejoice if there was wherewith they might blame us? Then they would triumph and rejoice indeed; and all your little slips, my dear brethren, are, and would be charged upon me. O at this time, when the eyes of so many are upon you, be upon your guard; and if you use the good things of this life with modera-tion, you do then celebrate this festival in the manner which the institution calls for.

And instead of running into excess, let that money, which you might expend to pamper your own bodies, be given to feed the poor; now, my brethren, is the season in which they commonly require relief; and sure you cannot act more agreeable, either to the season, to the time, or for the glory of God, than in relieving his poor distressed servants. Consider, Christ was always willing to relieve the distressed; it is his command also; and can you better commemorate the birth of your King, your Savior, the Lord Jesus Christ, than in obeying one of his commands?

Inquire strictly into your end and design in spending your time; see, my brethren, whether it proceeds from a true love to your Redeemer, or whether there is not some worldly pleasure or advantage at the bottom: if there is, our end is not right; but if it proceed entirely from love to him that died and gave himself for us, our actions will be a proof thereof; then our time will be spent, not in the polite pleasures of life, but according to the doctrine and commands of the blessed Jesus; then our conversation will be in heaven; and O that this might be found to be the end of each of you who now hear me; then we should truly observe this festival and have a true regard to the occasion thereof, that of Christ's coming to redeem the souls of those which were lost.

Let me now conclude, my dear brethren, with a few words of exhortation, beseeching you to think of the love of the Lord Jesus Christ. Did Jesus come into the world to save us from death, and shall we spend no part of our time in conversing about our dear Jesus; shall we pay no regard to the birth of him who came to redeem us from the worst of slavery, from that of sin, and the devil; and shall this Jesus not only be born on our account, but likewise die in our stead, and yet shall we be unmindful of him? Shall we spend our time in those things which are offensive to him? Shall we not rather do all we can to promote his glory and act according to his command?

O my dear brethren, be found in the ways of God; let us not disturb our dear Redeemer by any irregular proceedings; and let me beseech you to strive to love, fear, honor, and obey him, more than ever you have done yet; let not the devil engross your time, and that dear Savior who came into the world on your accounts have so little. O be not so ungrateful to him who has been so kind to you! What could the Lord Jesus Christ have done for you more than he has? Then do not abuse his mercy, but let your time be spent in thinking and talking of the love of Jesus, who was incarnate for us, who was born of a woman, and made under the law, to redeem us from the wrath to come.

Adapted from "The Observation of the Birth of Christ, the Duty of all Christians; or the True Way of Keeping Christmas," sermon (16) by George Whitefield, in *Selected Sermons of George Whitefield*.

2

Tabernacled among Us

JOSEPH "SKIP" RYAN

"And the Word became flesh and dwelt among us, and we have seen his glory, glory as of the only Son from the Father, full of grace and truth."

John 1:14

When a person makes his home among people, he moves in with them. He identifies with them. The incarnation is the moving in of the eternal Word so that he utterly identifies with us in every way. He took the whole nature of a human being, fully and totally identifying with all that it means for us to be human, including that which psychologists tell us is the most traumatic event of human life—birth.

A well-loved Christmas carol contains the line, "He abhors not the virgin's womb."[1] This should cause a bit of wonder and awe. The eternal God of all the universe did not abhor a virgin's womb. How messy!

Thousands of years before Jesus, God purposed that there be a tabernacle in order that there would be One who would fulfill the meaning of that tabernacle, who would be the true Tabernacle for us.

I assisted with the delivery of two of our children. A few minutes before Christopher, our first child, was born, Barbara's obstetrician asked, "Do you want to do this?"

I said, "Sure."

He said, "Wash up." And I did. I delivered Christopher, and two years later I delivered Carey. I thought I might drop her, she was so slippery. Birth is messy! What a wonder that the eternal Word of God did not shun being born.

It had to happen this way. Only in the complete identification with our flesh could Christ be the second Adam, the perfect man that Adam was not. Adam sinned and died as a man; only as a man could Jesus do what Adam failed to do and be the mediator between God and man. Why? Because only flesh can die.

The same truth is amplified in the next phrase of John 1:14, "the Word dwelt among us," literally, "tabernacled among us," which means, "he pitched a tent among us." The Old Testament tabernacle is where God moved in and lived with his people. This tabernacle had no meaning apart from Jesus Christ. Its whole purpose in the wilderness was to point people forward to the true Tabernacle who was to come, the Son of God. "For in Him all the fullness of Deity dwells in bodily form" (Col. 2:9).

Think about Jesus as the Tabernacle.

The tabernacle was for use in the wilderness: "Jesus was led up by the Spirit into the wilderness" (Matt. 4:1).

The tabernacle was outwardly humble and unattractive: "He has no stately form or majesty that we should look upon Him, nor appearance that we should be attracted to Him" (Isa. 53:2).

The tabernacle was where God met with men: "I am the way, and the truth, and the life; no one comes to the Father, but through Me" (John 14:6).

The tabernacle was the center of Israel's camp, a gathering place for God's people: "And I, if I be lifted up from the earth, will draw all men to Myself" (John 12:32).

The tabernacle was where sacrifices for the sins of God's people were made: "But He, having offered one sacrifice for sins for all time, sat down at the right hand of God" (Heb. 10:12).

The tabernacle was a place of worship: "My Lord and My God" (John 20:28).

We do not understand the teaching of the Old Testament in all of its fullness unless we read it through Jesus Christ—his incarnation, life, death, and resurrection. The tabernacle has absolutely no meaning apart from Jesus.

Thousands of years before Jesus, God purposed that there be a tabernacle in order that there would be One who would fulfill the meaning of that tabernacle, who would be the true Tabernacle for us. Just as the tabernacle in the wilderness contained and displayed God's glory (Ex. 40:34–35), even more do we behold "the glory of God in the face of Christ" (2 Cor. 4:6).

Moses sought to look upon the glory of God, and he was warned by God himself not to look (Ex. 33:18–20); but we have the privilege of looking upon the face of the Word of God, upon Jesus, by faith through his Word. Later, one day, by sight we will see the face of Jesus, who will be the full revelation of God and manifestation of his glory.

Glory means *weight* in the literal Hebrew. Many Christians today are into what we could call "Christian lite," like a "lite" beer. "Give me a little Jesus, just enough to make me happy." God thunders into our lives in his flesh and says that we behold in him the glory of God, full of grace and truth.

Grace? What is grace? Is it a sprinkling of fairy dust, a warm, happy feeling? No. Grace is a power that lifts you out of the domain of darkness and transfers you to the domain of light. Grace is God's magnificent power erupting in your heart and soul by his own intervention so that you move from death to life, from darkness to light, from hell to heaven. Grace is power that is embodied in a person.

What is truth? Twenty-five times in the Gospel of John we read about truth. Does truth mean "factual truth"? Yes, it does. "Objective truth"? Yes. But it means more than that; it also means truth that is embodied, infleshed. It means truth that is in the character of an individual. We find in Jesus Christ the One whose glory is displayed by the grace and the truth that he powerfully delivers to people.

Glory in the Gospel of John is used to describe the death of Christ. That is amazing. In John 12:23–24, for example, we read, "And Jesus answered them, saying, 'The hour has come for the Son of Man to be glorified. Truly, truly, I say to you, unless a grain of wheat falls into the earth and dies, it remains by itself alone; but if it dies, it bears much fruit.'" John Donne, in *The Book of Uncommon Prayers*, says, "The whole of Christ's life was a continual passion; others die martyrs, but Christ was born a martyr. He found a Golgotha, where he was crucified, even in Bethlehem, where he was born; for to his tenderness then the straws were almost as sharp as the thorns after, and the manger as uneasy at first as the cross at last. His birth and his death were but one continual act, and his Christmas Day and his Good Friday are but the evening and the morning of one and the same day. From the crèche to the cross is an inseparable line. Christmas only points forward to Good Friday and Easter. It can have no meaning apart from that, where the Son of God displayed his glory by his death."[2]

Grace is a person; Truth is a person—Jesus, come to you in the flesh.

Excerpted from *That You May Believe: New Life in the Son* by Joseph R. Ryan. Copyright © 2003 by Joseph R. Ryan. Used by permission of Crossway Books.

Scripture quotations are from *The New American Standard Bible*.

3

The Maiden Mary

MARTIN LUTHER

"In the sixth month the angel Gabriel was sent from God to a city of Galilee named Nazareth, to a virgin betrothed to a man whose name was Joseph, of the house of David. And the virgin's name was Mary. And he came to her and said, 'Greetings, O favored one, the Lord is with you!' But she was greatly troubled at the saying, and tried to discern what sort of greeting this might be. And the angel said to her, 'Do not be afraid, Mary, for you have found favor with God. And behold, you will conceive in your womb and bear a son, and you shall call his name Jesus. He will be great and will be called the Son of the Most High. And the Lord God will give to him the throne of his father David, and he will reign over the house of Jacob forever, and of his kingdom there will be no end.'"

Luke 1:26–33

The name of the maiden was <u>Mary. The Hebrew form of</u> the name is Miriam, and means <u>"bitter myrrh."</u> Why she was given this name I do not know, save that the Jews had the custom of naming children from the circumstances of the birth. Now the time when Christ should come was one of utter bitterness and extreme poverty for the Jews. They were a downtrodden people and their lot was pitiable, like ours today, so that all might well weep bitterly.

Among the downtrodden people she was one of the lowliest, not a maid of high station in the capital city, but a daughter of a plain man in a small town. We may infer that she was of no account because she herself said in her song, "He hath regarded the low estate of his handmaiden." Who knows whether Joachim and Anna, her parents, were alive at the time? In the village of Nazareth she appeared as a mere servant, tending the cattle and the house and no more esteemed that a maid among us who does her appointed chores. Her age was probably between thirteen and fifteen years.

And yet this was the one whom God chose. He might have gone to Jerusalem and picked out Caiaphas's daughter, who was fair, rich, clad in gold-embroidered raiment, and attended by a retinue of maids in waiting. But God preferred a lowly maid from a mean town.

Quite possibly Mary was doing the housework when the angel Gabriel came to her. Angels prefer to come to people as they are fulfilling their calling and discharging their office. The angel appeared to the shepherds as they were watching their flocks, to Gideon as he was threshing the grain, to Samson's mother as she sat in the field. Possibly, however, the Virgin Mary, who was very religious, was in a corner praying for the redemption of Israel. During prayer, also, the angels are wont to appear.

The angel greeted Mary and said, "Hail, Mary, full of grace." That is the Latin rendering, which unhappily has been taken over literally into German. Tell me, is this good German? Would any German say you are full of grace? I have translated it, "Thou gracious one," but if I were really to write German I would say, "God bless you, dear Mary—*liebe Maria*," for any German know that this word *liebe* comes right from the heart.

"Dear Mary," said the angel "the Lord is with you. Blessed are you among women." We are unable to tell whether Mary perceived at once that it was an angel who spoke to her. Luke seems to imply that she did not, because he indicates that she was abashed, not so much by his appearance, as by his words. And they were most unusual: "O Mary, you are blessed. You have a gracious God. No woman has ever lived on earth to whom God has shown such grace. You are the crown among them all." These words so overwhelmed the poor child that she did not know where she was. Then the angel comforted her and said: "Fear not, Mary, for you have found favor with God, and behold, you shall conceive in your womb and bring forth a son and you shall call his name Jesus. He shall be great and shall be called the Son of the Highest. And the Lord God shall give unto him the throne of his father David and he shall reign over the house of Jacob for ever; and of his kingdom there shall be no end."

She might have doubted, but she shut her eyes and trusted in God who could bring all things to pass, even though common sense were against it; and because she believed, God did to her as he had said.

To this poor maiden marvelous things were announced: that she should be the mother of the All Highest, whose name should be the Son of God. He would be a King and of his kingdom there would be no end. It took a mighty reach of faith to believe that this baby would play such a role. Well might Mary have said, "Who am I, little worm, that I should bear a King?" She might have doubted, but she shut her eyes and trusted in God who could bring all things to pass, even though common sense were against it; and because she believed, God did to her as he had said. She was indeed troubled at first and inquired, "How can these things be, seeing that I know not a man?" She was flesh and blood, and for that reason, the angel reassured her, saying, "The Holy Ghost shall come upon you, and the power of the Highest shall overshadow you, and therefore also that holy thing which shall be born of you shall be called the Son of God."

We must both read and meditate upon the nativity. If the meditation does not reach the heart, we shall sense no sweetness, nor shall we know what solace for humankind lies in this contemplation. The heart will not laugh nor be merry. As spray does not touch the deep, so mere meditation will not quiet the heart. There is such richness and goodness in this nativity that if we should see and deeply understand, we should be dissolved in perpetual joy.

The virgin birth is a mere trifle for God; that God should become man is a greater miracle.

Saint Bernard declared there are here three miracles: that God and man should be joined in this Child; that a mother should remain a virgin; that Mary should have such faith as to believe that this mystery would be accomplished in her. The last is not the least of the three. The virgin birth is a mere trifle for God; that God should become man is a greater miracle; but most amazing of all is that this maiden should credit the announcement that she, rather than some other virgin, had been chosen to be the mother of God. She did indeed inquire of the angel, "How can these things be?" and he answered, "Mary you have asked too high a question for me, but the Holy Spirit will come upon you and the power of the Most High will overshadow you and you will not know yourself how it happens." Had she not believed, she could not have conceived. She held fast to the word of the angel because she had become a new creature. Even so must we be transformed and renewed in heart from day to day. Otherwise Christ is born in vain.

This is the word of the prophet: "Unto us a child is born, unto us a son is given" (Isa. 9:6). This is for us the hardest point, not so much to believe that he is the son of the virgin and God himself, as to believe that this Son of God is ours. That is where we wilt, but he who does feel it has become another man. Truly it is marvelous in our eyes that God should place a little child in the lap of a virgin and that all our blessedness should lie in him. And this Child belongs to all mankind. God feeds the whole world through a Babe nursing at Mary's breast. This must be our daily exercise: to be transformed into Christ, being nourished by this food. Then will the heart be suffused with all joy and will be strong and confident against every assault.

Adapted from *Martin Luther's Christmas Book*, edited by Roland H. Bainton. Copyright © 1948 by W. L. Jenkins. Used by permission of Westminster John Knox Press.

Scripture quotations are from the King James Version.

4

Conceived by the Holy Spirit

JOHN PIPER

"And the angel said to her, 'Do not be afraid, Mary, for you have found favor with God. And behold, you will conceive in your womb and bear a son, and you shall call his name Jesus. He will be great and will be called the Son of the Most High. And the Lord God will give to him the throne of his father David, and he will reign over the house of Jacob forever, and of his kingdom there will be no end.'

And Mary said to the angel, 'How will this be, since I am a virgin?'

And the angel answered her, 'The Holy Spirit will come upon you, and the power of the Most High will overshadow you; therefore the child to be born will be called holy—the Son of God.'"

Luke 1:30–35

A recent book calls the Holy Spirit the shy member of the Trinity. His ministry is to point away from himself to the wonder of God the *Son* and God the *Father*. Being filled with the Spirit means being filled with love for *Christ*. When Jesus promised the Spirit (in John 16:14), he said, "He will glorify *me*, for he will take what is mine and declare it to you." The Spirit is shy; he is self-effacing. When we look toward him, he steps back and pushes forward Jesus Christ.

Therefore, in seeking to be filled and empowered by the Spirit we must pursue him indirectly—we must look to the wonder of Christ. If we look away from Jesus and seek the Spirit and his power directly, we will end up in the mire of our own subjective emotions. The Spirit does not reveal himself. The Spirit reveals Christ. The fullness of the Spirit is the fullness that he gives as we gaze on Christ. The power of the Spirit is the power we feel in the presence of Christ. The joy of the Spirit is the joy we feel from the promises of Christ. Many of us know what it is to crouch on the floor and cry out to the Holy Spirit for joy and power, and experience nothing; but the next day devote ourselves to earnest meditation on the glory of *Jesus Christ* and be filled with the Spirit.

Devote yourselves to seeing and feeling the grandeur of the love of God in Jesus Christ and you will be so in harmony with the Holy Spirit that his power will flow mightily in your life. Christian spiritual experience is not a vague religious emotion. It is an emotion with objective content, and the content is Jesus Christ. The shy member of the Trinity does mighty work, but he never puts himself in the limelight. You might say he *is* the limelight that puts the attributes of God the Father and the person of Christ into sharp relief.

Therefore, when the time came for the eternal Son of God to be sent by his Father into the world, the work of the Holy Spirit was a quiet, unobtrusive work in the service of the Father and the Son. Through him the Father caused the Son to be conceived in Mary the virgin. So from the very beginning of Christ's incarnation the Holy Spirit was quietly doing what needed to be done to put forward Jesus Christ as the Son of God and Savior of man. . . .

"The angel said to her, 'Do not be afraid, Mary, for you have found favor with God. And behold, you will conceive in your womb and bear a son, and you shall call his name Jesus. He will be great and will be called Son of the Most High. And the Lord God will give to him the throne of his father David, and he will reign over the house of Jacob forever, and of his kingdom there will be no end.'" This is where the shy member of the Trinity (who inspired this Scripture) does his best work. He magnifies Jesus, not himself.

His name will be Jesus. In Hebrew: Joshua, which means Savior or Deliverer. Gabriel loves to highlight grace. Before he tells Mary of Christ's greatness and dignity and power, he tells her how he is going to use this greatness and dignity and power. He is going to use it as a Savior. So don't be afraid, Mary, your child will be your Savior. He will be *Jesus.*

"He will be great" (v. 32). Jesus is great. He is very great. A Christian who feels ashamed of Jesus Christ is like a candle feeling ashamed of the sun. Our Lord Jesus has been "appointed the heir of all things, through whom also [God] created the world. He is the radiance of the glory of God and the exact imprint of his nature, and he upholds the universe by the word of his power" (Heb. 1:2–3). Is there anything great in the world that excites you, that you go out of your way to see or hear? Christ made it! And he is ten million times greater in every respect, except sin. If you took all the greatest thinkers of every country and every century of the world and put them in a room with Jesus, they would shut their mouths and listen to the greatness of his wisdom. All the greatest generals would listen to his strategy.

From the very beginning of Christ's incarnation the Holy Spirit was quietly doing what needed to be done to put forward Jesus Christ as the Son of God and Savior of man.

All the greatest musicians would listen to his music theory and his performance on every instrument. There is nothing that Jesus cannot do a thousand times better than the person you admire most in any area of human endeavor under the sun. Words fail to fill the greatness of Jesus.

If the heartbeat of your life is the glory of Jesus Christ, the Spirit will empower and help you with all his might.

Gabriel says he "will be called Son of the Most High." It's true that disciples of Jesus are also called "sons of the Most High" (Luke 6:35) and so some say that the sonship of Jesus is not anything more than what you or I have. I doubt that for two reasons. One is that Gabriel is giving a description of what distinguishes Jesus: he is great, he is king, he is eternal. It would be pointless and out of place to say: he is merely a son of God by faith like you and me. The other reason is that in Luke 8:28 a demon cries to Jesus, "What have you to do with me, Jesus, Son of the Most High God? I beg you, do not torment me." The demons recognize that Jesus' sonship is not like ours. As the Son of God he has the right and power to torment the forces of Satan. So Gabriel means: Jesus is uniquely God's Son, the divine Word and image of God, begotten from all eternity.

Gabriel says, "The Lord God will give to him the throne of his father, David." Since Mary's son will be the Savior of his people, will be superior in greatness, and will be called the Son of the Most High, it is fitting and inevitable that he will be king. He will fulfill all the prophecies that a son of David will rule over Israel. But not only over Israel. Isaiah 11:10 says, "In that day the root of Jesse, who shall stand as a signal for the peoples—of him shall the *nations* inquire, and his resting place shall be glorious" (cf. Luke 2:32). Mary's son will some day rule the *world* (Luke 2:32).

Gabriel says, "He will reign over the house of Jacob forever, and of his kingdom there will be no end." Do you see what this promise means? It means that Jesus is alive and ruling over his people right now, today. Do you believe that? Jesus, Savior, Son of God, King of the world, is governing. If Gabriel has spoken the truth, *the issue* right now, no matter where you live on this planet, is: Will you bow before the kingship of Jesus and obey the rule of his kingdom?

Now Mary catches her breath, and instead of mocking the impossible, she humbly asks (in v. 34), "How will this be, since I am a virgin?" She was ready to believe that she might give birth to the Messiah, but that she might give birth as a virgin was beyond comprehension. But her attitude was humble and open and so Gabriel answered her as far as he was allowed. Verse 35: "The Holy Spirit will come upon you, and the power of the Most High will overshadow you; therefore the child to be born will be called holy—the Son of God." Gabriel's answer to Mary's question, how? is very simply and delicately: *the Holy Spirit*. Beyond this, revelation does not go. How can a virgin have a child? How can the human child be the divine Son of God? Answer: "The Holy Spirit will come upon you . . . *therefore* the child to be born will be called . . . the Son of God." The word "therefore" in Luke 1:35 is tremendously important. It shows that the conception of Jesus in a virgin is owing to the mysterious work of the Holy Spirit. And it shows that the divine sonship of Jesus depends on his virgin birth.

Many people will try to say that the conception of Jesus Christ by the Holy Spirit in the virgin Mary is not essential in the doctrine of the incarnation, since Jesus would have been the Son of God even if the virgin birth weren't true. The words of Gabriel do not agree. In answer to the question, how can a virgin conceive? he says, "The Holy Spirit will come upon you and the power of the Most High will overshadow you, *therefore* the child to be born will be called holy—the *Son of God*." Jesus can be called Son of God (v. 35), Son of the Most High (v. 32), precisely because he was "conceived by the

Holy Spirit, born of the Virgin Mary." It is an unfathomable mystery that all the fullness of deity should dwell bodily in Jesus (Col. 2:9). It is fitting (indeed necessary, I think) that the entrance gate to this mystery of incarnation should be the virgin birth. And it should cause us to smile with pleasure that the shy member of the Trinity should be assigned the delicate and wonderful and mysterious work of causing the virgin to conceive—to conceive the One whose greatness he will magnify for ever. It's all so beautifully appropriate.

In verses 36 and 37 Gabriel gives the pregnancy of barren Elizabeth as evidence for Mary that "nothing will be impossible with God." The Holy Spirit may be shy, but he is also omnipotent. What a tribute to Jesus Christ that an omnipotent member of the Trinity exists to magnify his greatness.

Mary responds by saying, "Behold, I am the servant of the Lord; let it be to me according to your word" (v. 38). Can you say: "Let the Holy Spirit do with me as he pleases"? Do you trust the Spirit enough to say: "I am your slave; take me; use your omnipotent power to put me *where* you want me, *when* you want me there, doing *what* you want me to do"? Do you know why we can entrust ourselves to the Holy Spirit? Because he exists to exalt the glory of Jesus Christ. Therefore, if the heartbeat of your life is the glory of Jesus Christ, the Spirit will empower and help you with all his might.

Let's live and speak so that men and women might know that Jesus Christ is a great Savior, the Son of the Most High, and the never-ending King of kings. That's the passion of the Holy Spirit. To be full of that is to be full of him.

Adapted from "Christ Conceived by the Holy Spirit," sermon by John Piper, Bethlehem Baptist Church, Minneapolis, March 11, 1984. The complete text of this sermon is available at: http://www.desiringgod.org/ResourceLibrary/Sermons/ByDate/1984/429_Christ_Conceived_by_the_Holy_Spirit/. Used by permission.

Scripture quotations are from the English Standard Version.

5

The Gifts of Christmas

TIM KELLER

"In those days Mary arose and went with haste into the hill country, to a town in Judah, and she entered the house of Zechariah and greeted Elizabeth. And when Elizabeth heard the greeting of Mary, the baby leaped in her womb. And Elizabeth was filled with the Holy Spirit, and she exclaimed with a loud cry, 'Blessed are you among women, and blessed is the fruit of your womb! And why is this granted to me that the mother of my Lord should come to me? For behold, when the sound of your greeting came to my ears, the baby in my womb leaped for joy. And blessed is she who believed that there would be a fulfillment of what was spoken to her from the Lord.'"

Luke 1:39–45

What God gave us at Christmas was not just his Son. He gave us a Truth—a Truth that transforms us when we take it in. What God gave us at Christmas is a whole new life.

In the first chapter of Luke, Elizabeth says, "Blessed is she who has believed that what the Lord has said to her will be accomplished" (NIV). Elizabeth is saying to Mary—and to us—"if you really believe what the angel told you about this baby, if you take it in, you'll be blessed."

But our English word "blessed" is so limp and lightweight. In English we use blessed to mean something like "inspired." But in the Hebrew and Greek Scriptures, the word for blessed meant something much deeper than that. To be blessed brings you back to full *shalom*, full human functioning; it makes you everything God meant for you to be. To be blessed is to be strengthened and repaired in every one of your human capacities, to be utterly transformed.

What Elizabeth is saying to Mary, and what Luke is saying to us is, "Do you believe that this beautiful idea of the incarnation will really happen? If you believe it, and if you will take it into the center of your life, you're blessed, transformed, utterly changed."

When we open the package of Christmas, we find God has given us many gifts—vulnerability for intimacy, comfort for suffering, passion for justice, and power over prejudice.

In all relationships—marriage, parent-child, co-worker—at some point you get into a conversation that goes something like this:

"You're to blame!"

"No, it's your fault!"

"No, it's you."

"No, it isn't. It's you."

What's happening? The relationship is falling apart because neither side will take the blame, budge an inch, or make any concessions. Neither side will admit wrong or drop defenses. And as long as defenses are up, the relationship is going awry.

But then sometimes this happens:

"You're to blame!"

"No, it's your fault!"

"No, it's you."

"No, it isn't. It's you."

"Okay, it's me."

One person drops defenses. The relationship starts to come back because one person is willing to say, "Yeah, it's me. I am to blame here." One person makes himself or herself vulnerable, and the relationship is restored. In fact, it often becomes deeper and more intimate than it was before.

In the gift of Christmas, the unassailable, omnipotent God became a baby, giving us the ultimate example of letting our defenses down.

Why would a person do that? Because in the midst of all the yelling and all the hostility, one person decides that despite how distorted the other person has become because of anger, he wants the other person back. He wants the relationship to be restored.

The only way to do that is take down the shield, become vulnerable, and let one of the verbal blows land. It hurts, but it's the only way. It's a costly act of redemption for the relationship. And it works because we are created in the image of the One who gave the ultimate expression of this part of his own nature at Christmas.

In the gift of Christmas, the unassailable, omnipotent God became a baby, giving us the ultimate example of letting our defenses down. C. S. Lewis put it like this,

> Love anything and your heart will be wrung and possibly broken. If you want to make sure of keeping it intact, you must give it to no one, not even an animal. Wrap it carefully round with hobbies and little luxuries; avoid all entanglements. Lock it up safe in the casket or coffin of your selfishness. But in that casket, safe, dark, motionless, airless, it will change. It will not be broken; it will

become unbreakable, impenetrable, irredeemable. To love is to be vulnerable.[1]

There is no way to have a real relationship without becoming vulnerable to hurt. And Christmas tells us that God became breakable and fragile. God became someone we could hurt. Why? To get us back.

And if you believe this and take it into your life, you're blessed. As you take in the truth of what he did for you—how loved and affirmed you are—you'll be able to let down your defenses in your own relationships with other people. You won't always need to guard your honor. You'll be able to let down the barriers down. You'll be able to move into intimate relationships with other people.

What is in the package of Christmas? His vulnerability for intimacy with us, which gives us the vulnerability to be intimate with the people around us.

If you believe in Christmas—that God became a human being—you have an ability to face suffering, a resource for suffering that others don't have.

When September 11th happened and New Yorkers started to suffer, you heard two voices. You heard the conventional moralistic voices saying, "When I see you suffer, it tells me about a judging God. You must not be living right, and so God is judging you." When they see suffering, they see a judgmental God.

The secular voice said, "When I see people suffering, I see God is missing." When they see suffering, they see an absent, indifferent God.

But when we see Jesus Christ dying on the cross through an act of violence and injustice, what kind of God do we see then? A condemning God? No, we see a God of love paying for sin. Do we see a missing God? Absolutely not! We see a God who is not remote but involved.

We sometimes wonder why God doesn't just end suffering. But we know that whatever the reason, it isn't one of indifference or remoteness. God so hates suffering and evil that he was willing to come into it and become enmeshed in it.

Dorothy Sayers wrote,

> For whatever reason, God chose to make man as he is—limited and suffering and subject to sorrows and death—he [God] had the honesty and the courage to take his own medicine. Whatever game he is playing with his creation, he has kept his own rules and played fair. He can exact nothing from man that he has not exacted from himself. He has himself gone through the whole of human experience, from the trivial irritations of family life and the cramping restrictions of hard work and lack of money to the worst horrors of pain and humiliation, defeat, despair, and death. When he was a man, he played the man. He was born in poverty and died in disgrace, and thought it was worthwhile.[2]

The gift of Christmas gives you a resource—a comfort and consolation—for dealing with suffering, because in it we see God's willingness to enter this world of suffering to suffer with us and for us.

No other religion—whether secularism, Greco-Roman paganism, Eastern religion, Judaism, or Islam—believes God became breakable or suffered or had a body.

Eastern religion believes the physical is illusion. Greco-Romans believe the physical is bad. Judaism and Islam don't believe God would do such a thing as live in the flesh.

But Christmas teaches that God is concerned not only with the spiritual, because he is not just a spirit anymore. He has a body. He knows what it's like to be poor, to be a refugee, to face persecution and hunger, to be beaten and stabbed. He knows what it is like to be dead. Therefore, when we put together the incarnation and the resurrection, we see that God is not just concerned about the spirit, but he also cares about the body. He created the spirit and the body, and he will redeem the spirit and the body.

Christmas shows us that God is not just concerned about spiritual problems but physical problems too. So we can talk about redeeming people from guilt and unbelief, as well as creating safe streets and affordable housing for the poor, in the same breath. Because Jesus himself is not just a spirit but also has a body, the gift of Christmas is a passion for justice.

There are a lot of people in this world who have a passion for justice and a compassion for the poor but have absolutely no assurance that justice will one day triumph. They just believe that if we work hard enough long enough, we'll pull ourselves together and bring some justice to this world. For these people, there's no consolation when things don't go well.

Christmas is the end of thinking you are better than someone else, because Christmas is telling you that you could never get to heaven on your own. God had to come to you.

But Christians have not only a passion for justice but also the knowledge that, in the end, justice will triumph. Confidence in the justice of God makes the most realistic passion for justice possible.

Lastly, in the package of Christmas, there's the ability to reconnect with the part of the human race you despise.

Have you ever noticed how women-centric the incarnation and resurrection narratives are? Do you realize that women, not men, are at the very center of these stories?

For example, in the story of the resurrection, who was the only person in the world who knew that Jesus Christ had risen from the dead? Mary Magdelene, a former mental patient, is the one Jesus tells to take this news to the world. Everyone else in the whole world learns it from her. Women are the first people to see Jesus risen from the dead.

In the incarnation, the annunciation comes to a woman. God penetrates the world through the womb of a poor, unwed, Jewish, teenage girl. The first theological reflection group trying to wrap their minds around this to figure out what this means and what is going on is Mary and Elizabeth.

We know that in those days women had a very, very low status. They were marginalized and oppressed. For example, we know that a woman's testimony was not admissible in court. Why? Because of prejudice against women.

We say to ourselves, *aren't we glad we're past all that?* Yes, but here's what we have to realize: God is deliberately working with people the world despises. The very first witnesses to his nativity and resurrection are people whom the world says you can't trust, people the world looks down on.

Because we don't look down on women today, we don't look at this part of the story and realize what we're being told. But here's what we're being told: Christmas is the end of snobbishness. Christmas is the end of thinking, *Oh, that kind of person.*

You don't despise women, but you despise somebody. (Oh, yes you do!) You may not be a racist, but you certainly despise racists. You may not be a bigot, but you have certain people about which you think, *They're the reason for the problems in the world.*

There's a place in one of Martin Luther's nativity sermons where he asks something like, "Do know what a stable smells like? You know what that family would have smelled like after the birth when they went out into the city? And if they were standing next to you, how would you have felt about them and regarded them?" He is saying, *I want you to see Christ in the neighbor you tend to despise—in the political party you despise, in the race you despise, in the class of people you despise.*

Christmas is the end of thinking you are better than someone else, because Christmas is telling you that you could never get to heaven on your own. God had to come to you. It is telling you that people who are saved are not those who have arisen through their own ability to be what God wants them to be. Salvation comes to those who are willing to admit how weak they are.

In Christmas there is a resource for something most of us don't even feel the need of. We might be able to admit we have trouble being vulnerable or that we need help handling suffering or that we need more passion for justice. But almost nobody says, "What am I going to do about my prejudice and snobbery? I really need help with that."

Do you remember what an incredible snob you were when you were a teenager? Teenagers generally want nothing to do with people who don't dress right and look cool. Do you think you ever got over that? You're not really over that. You just found more socially acceptable ways to express it. You see, teenagers let that aspect of human nature out and don't realize how stupid they look, and after a while they get rid of it. But really they are just papering over it. There are all kinds of people you look down on and want nothing to do with—and you know it. But in Christmas you have this amazing resource to decimate that—to remove it and take it away.

These are the gifts that come in the package of Christmas—vulnerability for intimacy, strength for suffering, passion for justice, and power over prejudice. And you are blessed if you open this gift and take it into your life. If you do, you'll be blessed. You'll be transformed.

Adapted from "Mary," sermon by Tim Keller, Redeemer Presbyterian Church, New York, December 23, 2001. Copyright © by Timothy Keller, 2007. All rights reserved. Used by permission.

Scripture quotations are from the New International Version.

6

The Great Fulfillment

MARTYN LLOYD-JONES

"He has helped his servant Israel,
    in remembrance of his mercy,
as he spoke to our fathers,
    to Abraham and to his offspring forever."

Luke 1:54–55

The incarnation is the supreme example of fulfilled prophecy, the supreme example of God's faithfulness to his promises. And this is surely most comforting, especially as we consider it in the setting of the world in which we find ourselves.

The great covenant promise concerning redemption was made in its most explicit manner to Abraham. You can find it prior to that, but the definition of it, as it were, the explicit statement of it, is made to Abraham when he is told that in him, in his seed, shall all the world be blessed (Gen. 12:3). That is what Mary is referring to when she says: "He hath holpen his servant Israel, in remembrance of his mercy to Abraham, and to his seed for ever" (Luke 1:54, KJV).

Mary at once sees the significance of what is happening—the significance of the Son that is to be born out of her womb. She remembers what the archangel Gabriel said about him; she did not understand it then, but now she does, and she begins to realize the meaning of "He shall be great, and shall be called the Son of the Highest" (Luke 1:32, KJV). She begins to understand what Elisabeth means when she says, "Blessed art thou among women, and blessed is the fruit of thy womb. And whence is this to me, that the mother of my Lord should come to me?" (Luke 1:42–43, KJV).

She says in effect, "When I give birth to the Son, I am giving birth to the Savior, the one prophesied, predicted, promised. He is coming. All that was promised to Abraham, all this great mercy, here it is, literally coming into being and into action."

Mary sees now God is going to fulfill all these promises that he has made—"mercy to Abraham, and his seed forever." But how is it happening? "It happens," she said, "like this: 'He hath holpen his servant Israel,'" and that word means to succour, to help, or, perhaps better still, to lift up. The people of Israel had been cast down; they needed to be lifted up, they needed to be saved. They had been thrown down by an enemy, but someone comes and rescues them; he takes hold of them and helps them to stand upon their feet. So she says in effect, "When I give birth to the Son, I am giving birth to the Savior, the one prophesied, predicted, promised. He is coming. All that was promised to Abraham, all this great mercy, here it is, literally coming into being and into action."

She is referring primarily, of course, to salvation itself, and this is where her statement is so significant. God had made this promise to Abraham concerning salvation, forgiveness of sins, and reconciliation unto himself. We tend to forget that what God said to Abraham was that this salvation that was to come was to be brought about through this descendant of his that was yet to be born into this world. Now Abraham did not understand this fully; but he understood enough to rest his faith upon it. "He [Abraham] believed in the Lord; and he counted it to him for righteousness" (Gen 15:6, KJV).

Paul takes this up and works it out as a great argument in the fourth chapter of his epistle to the Romans, and also in the third chapter of the epistle to the Galatians. Our Lord himself also said to the Jews on one occasion, "Your father Abraham rejoiced to see my day: and he saw it, and was glad" (John 8:56, KJV). That is a reference to salvation. That statement means that Abraham was given to see, in a flash—not very clearly, but he saw it—that God's great salvation, the forgiveness of sins, and reconciliation was to be brought about ultimately by someone who would come into the world, who would be of his seed.

Mary is making a very basic statement here. "That," she says, "is what is happening." In other words, we have here a summary of the whole of the Old Testament, and nothing is more important than for us to realize that the whole of the Old Testament is looking forward to this event. The children of Israel were greatly blessed. They were God's own people. They were unlike all the other peoples and nations of the world, and God showered his blessings upon them.

But let us never make the mistake of imagining that they had everything. All they ultimately had was the promise. But it was enough. Thank God it was enough. But they had nothing more than that. You will find that this is frequently elaborated in the New Testament. There is that tremendous statement of it in Galatians 3; but you find it again in a striking manner in the epistle to the

Hebrews, at the end of that great eleventh chapter: "And these all, having obtained a good report through faith, received not the promise: God having provided some better thing for us, that they without us should not be made perfect (vv. 39–40, KJV). They did not receive the promise. What they received was the promise of the promise, the certainty that the promise would be fulfilled.

And here is the key, of course, to the understanding of the Old Testament. Look at those people as they went to their tabernacle and to their temple taking their burnt offerings and meal offerings and sacrifices—animals being killed, blood being shed and offered, placed before the alter, and so on. What is it all about? What was happening there? Well, the answer is, that was but a covering, as it were, of their sins for the time being. This argument is developed in the tenth chapter of Hebrews: "For it is not possible that the blood of bulls and of goats should take away sins" (v. 4, KJV). They were simply covered over. Those sacrifices were by types pointing to the coming of the great anti-type; they did not really deal with sin.

But they were indications that God had a way of dealing with sin, and that, says Mary, is what is now happening. Here are the promised mercies. God had promised Abraham and his seed that there would be mercy and compassion. Their sins would be forgiven and blotted out; they would be made the children of God and heirs of glory. But all that they knew by way of offerings and sacrifices was not the fulfillment of that. It was merely another way of giving the promise and of indicating in a measure the way in which it was going to be fulfilled.

But here now, says Mary, is the great anti-type himself. Now God is going to fulfill all this mercy that he had promised "to Abraham, and to his seed forever." And this means there is only one way of salvation; it means that all salvation and every aspect of it comes in this one way—in Jesus Christ, the Son of God and him crucified, made an offering for sin. "A body hast thou prepared me"(Heb. 10:5, KJV). What for? In order that he might be the Lamb of God. That he might be slain, that he might be offered. One sacrifice forever. "The Lamb of God, which taketh away the sin of the world!" (John 1:29, KJV).

That is what Mary is saying. Here is the fulfillment of all mercies. There is no forgiveness apart from Jesus Christ and him crucified. There is no true knowledge of God apart from him. There is no blessing apart from him. As the apostle Paul puts it in 2 Corinthians 1:20 (KJV): "For all the promises of God in him are yea, and in him Amen, unto the glory of God by us." "He hath holpen his servant Israel." Israel is the seed of Abraham. Yes, but under the law and condemned by the law. Not able to be free; held in bondage and in captivity; living on the promises, thank God, but nothing more.

What God did when he sent his Son into the world is an absolute guarantee that he will do everything he has ever promised to do.

But here is the great fulfillment; and so you will find all the Old Testament prophets, psalmists, and seers have seen this. They are looking forward; they know that this is what will fulfill all the promises and bring the mercy into the individual experience. It is all in and through our Lord and Savior Jesus Christ and what he did when he was in this world, and what he is now continuing and applying in the glory.

What God did when he sent his Son into the world is an absolute guarantee that he will do everything he has ever promised to do. Look at it in personal sense: "All things work together for good to them that love God"—that is a promise—"to them who are the called according to his purpose" (Rom. 8:28, KJV). "But how can I know that is true for me?" asks someone. The answer is the incarnation. God has given the final proof that all his promises are sure, that he is faithful to everything he has ever said. So that promise is sure for you. Whatever your state or condition may be, whatever may happen to you, he has said, "I will never leave thee, nor forsake thee" (Heb. 13:5, KJV)—and he will not. He has said so, and we have absolute proof that he fulfills his promises. He does not always do it immediately in the way that we think. No, no! But he does it! And he will never fail to do it.

7

Joseph: Righteous and Kind

J. LIGON DUNCAN III

"Now the birth of Jesus Christ took place in this way. When his mother Mary had been betrothed to Joseph, before they came together she was found to be with child from the Holy Spirit. And her husband Joseph, being a just man and unwilling to put her to shame, resolved to divorce her quietly. But as he considered these things, behold, an angel of the Lord appeared to him in a dream, saying, 'Joseph, son of David, do not fear to take Mary as your wife, for that which is conceived in her is from the Holy Spirit. She will bear a son, and you shall call his name Jesus, for he will save his people from their sins.' All this took place to fulfill what the Lord had spoken by the prophet:

'Behold, the virgin shall conceive and bear a son,
    and they shall call his name Immanuel'

(which means, God with us). When Joseph woke from sleep, he did as the angel of the Lord commanded him: he took his wife, but knew her not until she had given birth to a son. And he called his name Jesus."

Matthew 1:18–25

Mary was betrothed to Joseph. This idea of betrothal is a somewhat foreign concept to us. Typically when we use the word "betroth," we are speaking of the wedding ceremony itself. For this reason, we tend to equate Mary's betrothal with engagement. Although that assumption is not entirely wrong, we must remember that betrothal in Israel was actually quite different from our modern-day engagement. A betrothal in Israel was much more final, much more committed, much more permanent, much more significant than our practice of modern engagement. When the Bible says that Mary was betrothed to Joseph, it means that the two of them had pledged in front of witnesses to be married to one another. Although they were neither living under the same roof, nor enjoying all of the privileges of being married, upon betrothal they were considered to be man and wife.

In Matthew 1:19, we learn of two crucial qualities possessed by Joseph; he was both a righteous and a kind man. When Joseph is met with the word that Mary is pregnant, despite them never having relations, he righteously determines to put her away. Joseph cares about the estate of matrimony. He loves the law of God and knows that the marriage bed is to be kept undefiled. Marriage is holy, and so Joseph will not trifle with it. Although he loves Mary, because of his love for God and his law, Joseph determines not to unite in an estate of adultery with this woman. So he decides to divorce her. He is going to gather the lawyers together to draw up the papers.

Joseph, however, reveals in the midst of this display of righteousness that he is a kind man. In spite of Joseph's wounded affections for Mary, he does not take the recourses of the law that were available to him. In the Old Testament, a betrothed woman found in adultery could have been stoned to death. Although this practice was not occurring in Israel during Joseph's time, Mary still could have been publicly disgraced and expelled from the community. But instead of publicly disgracing Mary, Joseph kindly determines to divorce her quietly.

The character of Joseph, the man God chose for his Son to have for an earthly father, is not only interesting, it is also instructive to us. There are many who are righteous, but who are not kind. There are many who are kind, but who are not righteous. Joseph, however, loved God and his law, and that love of God touched his heart, causing him to be a kind man. When God chose a human father for his Son, he chose a man who would be righteous and kind, qualities that reflect God the Father himself. Is that not instructive for every one of us to be like our heavenly Father, and to be like Jesus' earthly father? Righteous and kind. Concerned for God's law. Concerned for God's people.

In Matthew 1:20–21, God comes to Mary's rescue. Joseph thought she was guilty of some horrible infidelity, an infidelity that he could not even fathom. His heart must have been broken, so he determines to put her away. But as he is meditating, the angel of the Lord comes to Joseph in a dream saying, "Joseph, what you have thought is wrong. Your wife is innocent; she is pure. The child conceived in her is of the Holy Spirit. And she will bear the Savior."

When God chose a human father for his Son, he chose a man who would be righteous and kind, qualities that reflect God the Father himself.

Notice that God comes to Joseph as he is thinking, as he is meditating. We may assume that he is meditating on what God would have him do next. He is seeking guidance from God. As Matthew Henry says, "The Lord gives guidance to the thoughtful, not to the unthinking." God's guidance is not an excuse for us to check our brains at the door, or to cease thinking. Just as David meditated on the Word, Joseph is meditating on the Word and attempting to determine the honorable thing to do.

During this meditation, God comes to Joseph with guidance from the angel. Notice what the angel calls him, "the son of David."

God tells Joseph to take pregnant Mary and to take her as his wife, to accept that this pregnancy has come not from some shameful act on Mary's part, but through the miraculous work of the Holy Spirit. And that word would have seemed as shocking to Joseph as it would to us.

Joseph was a humble man, a carpenter. He was not a great land magnate, or a great merchant. He was not a famed man in his community. He did not hold public office. He was not some sort of nobility; yet the angel says, "Joseph, remember who you are. You are the son of David." Before God calls us to obey, before he calls us to a great task, he reminds us who we are in him. Although Joseph may not have been impressive in the eyes of the world, to God he was a son of David, the man after God's own heart; Joseph was a descendant of the great precursor of the messianic king. He was the son of David.

After reminding Joseph who he is, God instructs him: "Joseph, take Mary as your wife and name the boy Jesus." In verse 24, one of the most beautiful things is Joseph's obedience. Joseph awoke and did just as the Lord commanded. Joseph believed the Lord, trusted the Lord, and obeyed the Lord. What an enormous example of trust in spite of all evidence to the contrary! "Joseph, she hasn't been unfaithful. I know your heart is broken, and your head is muddled, but listen to me. Take her for your wife, and name the boy Jesus." And Joseph by faith does just as he is told.

What an example of trust and of obedience. You know the old gospel hymn by that same name: "Trust and obey, for there's no other way, to be happy in Jesus, but to trust and obey." And that is precisely what Joseph is doing. He takes God's revealed word, his authoritative word, even his difficult word, and he believes it, and he acts in obedience to it. God tells Joseph to take pregnant Mary and to take her as his wife, to accept that this pregnancy has come not from some shameful act on Mary's part, but through the miraculous work of the Holy Spirit. And that word would have seemed as shocking to Joseph as it would to us. Joseph understood where babies came from. God is not playing on Joseph's pre-scientific knowledge of anatomy and biology; God is calling Joseph to believe his word and to act in accordance with it. And Joseph does just that. He accepts God's word and he trusts God's word and he relies upon God's word and he re-orients his life to conform to that word. What a tremendous act of faith on the part of Joseph and what an example of obedience to God's word in spite of circumstance. It would have been, in many ways, easier for Joseph to disregard this word from God. He could have thought, *No way can I be expected to believe this thing which God has said. No way am I going to provide support and love to this child that is not from me. No way am I going to endure the smirks and questions about the timing of this pregnancy. It's too much, too hard.* No, instead, Joseph says, "Lord, I believe your word, and I am willing to do whatever it takes to be obedient to that word."

What do we learn in the circumstances of Jesus' birth? Among other things, we learn that the Lord comes and ministers guidance to his people as they reflect upon his Word. Furthermore, we learn that God calls us to justice and kindness, in order that we might mirror his image. Finally, we learn that trust and obedience after the manner of Joseph is the very way God intends us to walk.

Adapted from "Jesus' Virgin Birth: According to Scripture," sermon by Ligon Duncan III, First Presbyterian Church, Jackson, Mississippi, January 12, 1997. Used by permission.

8

To Be More Blessed Than Mary

JONATHAN EDWARDS

"As he said these things, a woman in the crowd raised her voice and said to him, 'Blessed is the womb that bore you, and the breasts at which you nursed!' But he said, 'Blessed rather are those who hear the word of God and keep it!'"

Luke 11:27–28

The great enquiry of the world in general in all ages of it, is after happiness. Yet there is scarce anything that the world is more deceived about. And thus therefore was no inconsiderable part of the errand of Jesus Christ, the great teacher of mankind, into the world, to instruct men wherein their true happiness consisted. He began his Sermon on the Mount with telling who were blessed.

The Jews, though they enjoyed the light of God's Word of the Old Testament, yet were generally deceived about it with the rest of the world. They imagined themselves happier than the rest of the world but placed their happiness in their external privileges in being the children of Abraham and Jacob, having the Law of Moses and being circumcised, and having the outward privilege of God's peculiar people, and being the nation from whence was to spring the Messiah according to God's promise.

In Luke 11, we have an account how a certain woman, as she heard Christ's heavenly discourses, was affected with admiration of his speeches and was convinced thereby that he was some wonderful person, and it may be was convinced that he was the Messiah. 'Tis given by some as a reason why the Israelite woman esteemed barrenness so great a calamity was the hope that every mother had of the Messiah descending from her or being of her posterity. And if it was esteemed so great a privilege to be the mother of the Messiah, no wonder that they considered the womb blessed that bore him and the paps that he had sucked.

But Christ tells her that they are rather blessed who hear the word of God. She seemed to admire that word of his that she heard that made her express herself so. Christ then instructs her that though her womb had not borne nor her paps given him suck, yet she might arrive at a greater blessedness than that of Mary by hearing and keeping the word of God. She had opportunity to hear his instructions and had now been hearing them. If she would not only hear but observe what she had heard, this would be greater blessedness.

How wonderful a privilege did God bestow on the blessed virgin Mary in making her the mother of Jesus Christ, the Son of God, the Creator of the world, and the Savior of sinners and the Judge of angels and men. How wonderful was the privilege that such a person should be conceived in her womb by the power of the Holy Ghost. Indeed she was highly favored and blessed among women as the angel told her in Luke 1:28, "Hail, thou that art highly favored, the Lord is with thee: blessed art thou among women."

In this account she is deservedly called the blessed virgin, as she herself says in her song in Luke 1:48–49: "For he hath regarded the low estate of his handmaiden: for, behold, from henceforth all generations shall call me blessed. For he that is mighty hath done to me great things; and holy is his name." Therefore Christ in our text doesn't deny what the woman says when she cries out, "Blessed is the womb that bare thee and the paps which thou hast sucked," but only that they are rather blessed who hear the word of God and keep it.

'Tis more blessed to be spiritually related to Jesus Christ—to be his disciples, his brethren and the members—than to stand in the nearest temporal relation, than to be his brother or his mother.

How great a privilege was it to this young virgin to conceive in her womb and hold in her arms and suckle at her breasts, a Child who was the Son of the highest, who was the great and eternal and infinitely beloved Son of God, the Creator and mighty Governor of heaven and earth and the great Savior of mankind. Well might she say upon it, "My soul doth magnify the Lord and my spirit hath rejoiced in God my Savior."

But hearing and keeping the word of God renders a person more blessed than any of those privileges. By "hearing the Word of God" is either intended an external or an internal or spiritual hearing. The woman to whom Christ directed himself in the text had been hearing the word externally. Christ therefore here informs her that if she not only hears but keeps this word, he will render her more blessed than that privilege that she spoke of.

The inward and spiritual hearing the word of God includes these three things:

1. A spiritual understanding of it, as hearing the great and wonderful things contained in it and the excellency of it revealed by the Spirit of God to the soul.

2. So in spiritual hearing is implied a following the word, a receiving it as true and the things which it reveals, as real and certain things.

3. Hereby is implied the yielding of the heart and inclination to it. In this spiritual hearing there is not only an assent of the understanding, but the consent of the will.

By keeping the word of God is meant:

1. A strict and careful observation of it in practice, a living according to the word of God, an observing the doctrine of the word of God, to be swayed and governed by them in life and observing the precepts of the word of God to perform them.

2. To never lose or cast away or forsake God's word, nor any one known command of it but keep it to the end.

The hearing and keeping the word of God brings the happiness of a spiritual union and communion with God. 'Tis a greater blessedness to have spiritual communion with God and

'Tis more blessed to have Christ in the heart than in the womb.

to have a saving intercourse with him by the instances of his Spirit and by the exercise of true devotion than it is to converse with God externally, to see the visible representation and manifestations of his presence and glory, and to hear his voice with the bodily ears as Moses did. For in this spiritual intercourse the soul is nigh unto and hath more a particular portion than in any external intercourse.

'Tis more blessed to be spiritually related to Jesus Christ—to be his disciples, his brethren and the members—than to stand in the nearest temporal relation, than to be his brother or his mother.

Matthew 12:47–50 says, "Then one said unto him, Behold, thy mother and thy brethren stand without, desiring to speak with thee. But he answered and said unto him that told him, Who is my mother? and who are my brethren? And he stretched forth his hand toward his disciples, and said, Behold my mother and my brethren! For whosoever shall do the will of my Father which is in heaven, the same is my brother, and sister, and mother." They are his mother and sister or brother in a more excellent and blessed sense. They who hear the word of God and keep it, do as it were conceive and bring forth Christ in the heart. Christ is formed in them. Galatians 4:19 says, "My little children, of whom I travail in birth again until Christ be formed in you."

'Tis more blessed to have Christ in the heart than in the womb. 'Tis more blessed to have Christ in the arms of faith and love than in the arms or at the breast as the virgin Mary had.

Adapted from "That Hearing and Keeping the Word of God Renders a Person More Blessed Than Any Other Privilege That Ever God Bestowed on Any of the Children of Men" by Jonathan Edwards, in *The Glory and Honor of God: Volume 2 of the Previously Unpublished Sermons of Jonathan Edwards,* edited by Michael D. McMullen. Copyright © 2004 by Michael McMullen. Used by permission of Broadman & Holman.

Scripture quotations are from the King James Version.

9

Have You Any Room?

CHARLES SPURGEON

"And she gave birth to her firstborn son and wrapped him in swaddling cloths and laid him in a manger, because there was no place for them in the inn."

Luke 2:7

When all persons of the house of David were thus driven to Bethlehem, the scanty accommodation of the little town would soon be exhausted. Doubtless friends entertained their friends till their houses were all full, but Joseph had no such willing kinsmen in the town. There was the caravanserai, which was provided in every village, where free accommodation was given to travelers; this, too, was full, for coming from a distance and compelled to travel slowly, the humble couple had arrived late in the day. The rooms within the great brick square were already occupied with families; there remained no better lodging, even for a woman in travail, than one of the meaner spaces appropriated to beasts of burden. The stall of the ass was the only place where the child could be born. By hanging a curtain at its front and perhaps tethering the animal on the outer side to block the passage, the needed seclusion could be obtained, and here, in the stable, was the King of Glory born and in this manner was he laid.

The palaces of emperors and the halls of kings afforded the royal stranger no refuge? Alas! my brethren, seldom is there room for Christ in palaces! State chambers, cabinets, throne rooms, and royal palaces are about as little frequented by Christ as the jungles and swamps of India by the cautious traveler. He frequents cottages far more often than regal residences, for there is no room for Jesus Christ in regal halls.

But there were senators, there were forums of political discussion, there were the places where the representatives of the people make the laws—was there no room for Christ there? Alas! my brethren, none, and to this day there is very little room for Christ in parliaments. Parties, policies, place-hunters, and pleasure-seekers exclude the Representative of heaven from a place among representatives of Earth.

Might there not be found some room for Christ in what is called good society? Were there not in Bethlehem some people that were very respectable, who kept themselves aloof from the common multitude; persons of reputation and standing—could not they find room for Christ? Ah! dear friends, it is too much the case that there is no room for him in what is called good society. Folly and finery, rank and honor, jewels and glitter, frivolity and fashion, all report that there is no room for Jesus in their abodes.

But is there not room for him on the exchange? Cannot he be taken to the marts of commerce? Here are the shopkeepers of a shopkeeping nation—is there not room for Christ here? Ah! dear friends, how little of the spirit, and life, and doctrine of Christ can be found here! Bankruptcies, swindlings, and frauds are so abundant that in hosts of cases there is no room for Jesus in the mart or the shop.

Then there are the schools of the philosophers, surely they will entertain him. No, dear friends, but it is not so; there is very little room for Christ in colleges and universities, very little room for him in the seats of learning. A few with splendid talents, a few of the erudite and profound have bowed like children at the feet of the Babe of Bethlehem and have been honored in bowing there, but too many, conscious of their knowledge, stiff and stern in their conceit of wisdom, have said, "Who is Christ, that we should acknowledge him?"

If thou hast but room for Christ he will come and be thy guest.

But there was surely one place where he could go—it was the Sanhedrin, where the elders sit. Or could he not be housed in the priestly chamber where the priests assemble with the Levites? Was there not room for him in the temple or the synagogue? No, he found no shelter there; it was there, his whole life long, that he found his most ferocious enemies. There is no room for him where his name is chanted in solemn hymns and his image lifted up amid smoke of incense. Go where ye will, and there is no space for the Prince of peace but with the humble and contrite spirits which by grace he prepares to yield him shelter.

As the palace, and the forum, and the inn, have no room for Christ, and as the places of public resort have none, have you room for Christ?

"Well," says one, "I have room for him, but I am not worthy that he should come to me." Ah! I did not ask about worthiness; have you room for him? "Oh! but I feel it is a place not at all fit for Christ!" Nor was the manger a place fit for him, and yet there was he laid. "Oh! but I have been such a sinner; I feel as if my heart had been a den of beasts and devils!" Well, the manger had been a place where beasts had fed. Have you room for him? Never mind what the past has been; he can forget and forgive. It mattereth not what even the present state may be if thou mournest it. If thou hast but room for Christ he will come and be thy guest.

Do not say, I pray you, "I hope I shall have room for him"; the time is come that he shall be born; Mary cannot wait months and years. Oh! sinner, if thou hast room for him let him be born in thy soul today. "Today if ye will hear his voice, harden not your hearts, as in the provocation . . ." (Heb. 3:7–8). "Behold, now is the accepted time; behold, now is the day of salvation" (2 Cor. 6:2). Room for Jesus! Room for Jesus now!

"Oh!" saith one, "I have room for him, but will he come?" Will he come indeed! Do you but set the door of your heart open, do but say, "Jesus, Master, all unworthy and unclean I look to thee; come, lodge within my heart," and he will come to thee, and he will cleanse the manger of thy heart, nay, will transform it into a golden throne, and there he will sit and reign for ever and for ever.

My Master wants room! Room for him! Room for him! I, his herald, cry aloud, Room for the Savior! Room! Here is my royal Master—have you room for him? Here is the Son of God made flesh—have you room for him? Here is he who can forgive all sin—have you room for him? Here is he who can take you up out of the horrible pit and out of the miry clay—have you room for him? Here is he who when he cometh in will never go out again, but abide with you forever to make your heart a heaven of joy and bliss for you—have you room for him?

'Tis all I ask. Your emptiness, your nothingness, your want of feeling, your want of goodness, your want of grace—all these will be but room for him.

'Tis all I ask. Your emptiness, your nothingness, your want of feeling, your want of goodness, your want of grace—all these will be but room for him. Have you room for him? Oh! Spirit of God, lead many to say, "Yes, my heart is ready." Ah! then he will come and dwell with you.

Adapted from "No Room for Christ in the Inn," sermon (485) by C. H. Spurgeon, Metropolitan Tabernacle, Newington, December 21, 1862. In *Metropolitan Tabernacle Pulpit*, vol. 8.

Scripture quotations are from the King James Version.

10

The Word Was Made Flesh

SAINT AUGUSTINE

"In the beginning was the Word, and the Word was with God, and the Word was God. He was in the beginning with God. . . . And the Word became flesh."

John 1:1–2, 14a

I n the beginning was the Word, and the Word was with God, and the Word was God" (John 1:1) O glorious preaching! Why seekest thou for what was before it? "In the beginning was the Word." If the Word had been made, the Scripture would have said, "In the beginning God made the Word"; as it is said in Genesis, "In the beginning God made the heaven and the earth" (Gen. 1:1). God then did not in the beginning make the Word, because, "In the beginning was the Word." This Word which was in the beginning, where was it? Follow on, "and the Word was with God."

But from our daily hearing the words of men we are wont to think lightly of this name of "Word." In this case do not think lightly of the name of "Word"; "the Word was God." The same, that is the Word, "was in the beginning with God. All things were made by him, and without him was nothing made."

He "was" before his own flesh; he created his own mother. He chose her in whom he should be conceived, he created her of whom he should be created.

Extend your hearts, help the poverty of my words. What I shall be able to express, give ear to; on what I shall not be able to express, meditate. Who can comprehend the abiding Word? All our words sound, and pass away. Who can comprehend the abiding Word, save he who abideth in him? Wouldest thou comprehend the abiding Word?

Do not follow the current of the flesh. For this flesh is indeed a current; for it has none abiding. As it were from a kind of secret fount of nature men are born, they live, they die; or whence they come, or whither they go, we know not. It is a hidden water, till it issue from its source; it flows on, and is seen in its course; and again it is hidden in the sea. Let us despise this stream flowing on, running, disappearing, let us despise it. "All flesh is grass, and all the glory of flesh is as the flower of grass. The grass withereth, the flower falleth away." Wouldest thou endure? "But the word of the Lord endureth for ever" (1 Pet. 1:24–25).

But in order to succour us, "The Word was made flesh, and dwelt among us" (John 1:14). What is, "the Word was made flesh"? The gold became grass. It became grass for to be burned; the grass was burned, but the gold remained; in the grass it perisheth not, yea, it changed the grass. How did it change it? It raised it up, quickened it, lifted it up to heaven, and placed it at the right hand of the Father.

"But how," one will say, "can it be, that the Word of God, by whom the world is governed, by whom all things both were and are created, should contract himself into the womb of a virgin; should leave the angels, and be shut up in one woman's womb?"

Thou skillest not to conceive of things divine. The Word of God could surely do all, seeing that the Word of God is omnipotent, at once remain with the Father, and come to us; at once in the flesh come forth to us, and lay concealed in him. For he would not the less have been, if he had not been born of flesh. He "was" before his own flesh; he created his own mother. He chose her in whom he should be conceived, he created her of whom he should be created. Why marvellest thou? It is God of whom I am speaking to thee: "the Word was God."

My word was with me, and it came forth into a voice: the Word of God was with the Father, and came forth into flesh. But can I do with my voice that which he could do with his flesh? For I am not master of my voice as it flies; he is not only master of his flesh, that it should be born, live, act; but even when dead he raised it up, and exalted unto the Father the vehicle as it were in which he came forth to us. You may call the flesh of Christ a garment, you may call it a vehicle, and as perchance himself vouchsafed to teach us, you may call it his beast; for on this beast he raised him who had been wounded by robbers. Lastly, as he said himself more expressly, you may call it a temple. This temple knows death no more. Its seat is at the right hand of the Father. In this temple shall he come to judge the quick and dead. What he hath by precept taught, he hath by example manifested. What he hath in his own flesh shown, that oughtest thou to hope for in thy flesh. This is faith; hold fast what as yet thou seest not. Need there is, that by believing thou abide firm in that thou seest not; lest when thou shalt see, thou be put to shame.

For I am not master of my voice as it flies; he is not only master of his flesh, that it should be born, live, act; but even when dead he raised it up, and exalted unto the Father the vehicle as it were in which he came forth to us.

Adapted from *St. Augustine: Homilies on the Gospel of John*, in *The Nicene and Post-Nicene Fathers*, First Series, vol. 7, edited by Philip Schaff, Sermon LXIX (CXIX Ben.).

11

For Your Sakes He Became Poor

J. I. PACKER

"For you know the grace of our Lord Jesus Christ, that though he was rich, yet for your sake he became poor, so that you by his poverty might become rich."

2 Corinthians 8:9

I t is here, in the thing that happened at the first Christmas, that the profoundest and most unfathomable depths of the Christian revelation lie. "The Word became flesh" (John 1:14); God became man; the divine Son became a Jew; the Almighty appeared on earth as a helpless human baby, unable to do more than lie and stare and wriggle and make noises. Needing to be fed and changed and taught to talk like any other child. And there was no illusion or deception in this; the babyhood of the Son of God was a reality. The more you think about it, the more staggering it gets. Nothing in fiction is so fantastic as is this truth of the incarnation.

How are we to think of the incarnation: The New Testament does not encourage us to puzzle our heads over the physical and psychological problems that it raises, but to worship God for the love that was shown in it. For it was a great act of condescension and self-humbling. "He, Who had always been God by nature," writes Paul, "did not cling to His prerogatives as God's equal, but stripped Himself of all privilege by consenting to be a slave by nature and being born as mortal man. And, having become man, He humbled Himself by living a life of utter obedience, even to the extent of dying, and the death he died was the death of a common criminal" (Phil. 2:6, PHILLIPS). And all this was for our salvation.

For the Christmas spirit is the spirit of those who, like their Master, live their whole lives on the principle of making themselves poor— spending and being spent—to enrich their fellow men, giving time, trouble, care, and concern, to do good to others— and not just their own friends—in whatever way there seems need.

The key text in the New Testament for interpreting the incarnation is not, therefore, the bare statement in John 1:14, "the Word became flesh and made his dwelling among us," but rather the more comprehensive statement of 2 Corinthians 8:9, "you know the grace of our Lord Jesus Christ, that though he was rich, yet for your sakes he became poor, so that you through his poverty might become rich." Here is stated, not the fact of the incarnation only, but also its meaning; the taking of manhood by the Son is set before us in a way that shows us how we should set it before ourselves and ever view it—not simply as a marvel of nature, but rather as a wonder of grace.

For the Son of God to empty himself and become poor meant a laying aside of glory; a voluntary restraint of power; an acceptance of hardship, isolation, ill-treatment, malice, and misunderstanding; finally, a death that involved such agony—spiritual, even more than physical—that his mind nearly broke under the prospect of it. It meant love to the uttermost for unlovely men, who "through his poverty, might become rich." This Christmas message is that there is hope for a ruined humanity—hope of pardon, hope of peace with God, hope of glory—because at the Father's will Jesus Christ became poor and was born in a stable so that thirty years later he might hang on a cross. It is the most wonderful message that the world has ever heard, or will hear.

We talk glibly of the "Christmas spirit," rarely meaning more by this than sentimental jollity on a family basis. But what we have said makes it clear that the phrase should in fact carry a tremendous weight of meaning. It ought to mean the reproducing in human lives of the temper of him who for our sakes became poor at the first Christmas. And the Christmas spirit itself ought to be the mark of every Christian all the year round.

It is our shame and disgrace today that so many Christians—I will be more specific: so many of the soundest and most orthodox Christians—go through this world in the spirit of the priest and the Levite in our Lord's parable, seeing human needs all around them, but (after a pious wish, and perhaps a prayer, that God might meet them) averting their eyes, and passing by on the other side. That is not the Christmas spirit. Nor is it the spirit of those Christians—alas, they are many—whose ambition in life seems limited to building a nice middle-class Christian home, and making nice middle-class Christian friends, and bringing up their children in nice middle-class Christian ways, and who leave the sub-middle-class sections of the community, Christian and non-Christian, to get on by themselves.

The Christmas spirit does not shine out in the Christian snob. For the Christmas spirit is the spirit of those who, like their Master, live their whole lives on the principle of making themselves poor—spending and being spent—to enrich their fellow men, giving time, trouble, care, and concern, to do good to others—and not just their own friends—in whatever way there seems need. There are not as many who show this spirit as there should be. If God in mercy revives us, one of the things he will do will be to work more of this spirit in our hearts and lives. If we desire spiritual quickening for ourselves individually, one step we should take is to seek to cultivate this spirit. "Ye know the grace of our Lord Jesus Christ, that though he was rich, yet for your sakes he became poor, that ye through his poverty might be rich." "Let this mind be in you, which was also in Christ Jesus." *"I run in the path of your commands, for you have set my heart free"* (Ps. 119:32).

12

Unto Us a Child Is Born

JOHN CALVIN

"For to us a child is born,
    to us a son is given;
and the government shall be upon his shoulder,
    and his name shall be called
Wonderful Counselor, Mighty God,
    Everlasting Father, Prince of Peace.
Of the increase of his government and of peace
    there will be no end,
on the throne of David and over his kingdom,
    to establish it and to uphold it
with justice and with righteousness
    from this time forth and forevermore.
The zeal of the Lord of hosts will do this."

Isaiah 9:6–7

A child is born. The Jews twist this passage and interpret it as relating to Hezekiah, though he had been born before this prediction was uttered. But Isaiah speaks of it as something new and unexpected; further, it is a promise, intended to arouse believers to the expectation of a future event. Therefore, there can be no hesitation in concluding that he is describing a child who was yet to be born.

Wonderful Counselor. Notice that these titles are not alien to the subject but are adapted to the case in hand, for the prophet describes what Christ will show himself to be toward believers. The redemption he has brought surpasses the creation of the world. It amounts to this: The grace of God, which will be exhibited in Christ, exceeds all miracles.

The Redeemer will come endowed with absolute wisdom. Let us remember that the prophet does not here reason about the hidden essence of Christ but about the power he displays toward us. It is not, therefore, because he knows all his Father's secrets that the prophet calls him Counselor, but rather because he is in every respect the highest and most perfect teacher. All that is necessary for salvation is opened up by Christ in such a way and explained with such familiarity that he addresses the disciples no longer as servants but as friends.

He is called Mighty God for the same reason that in Isaiah 7:14 he was called Immanuel. If in Christ we find nothing but human flesh and nature, our glorying will be foolish and vain, and our hope will rest on an uncertain and insecure foundation. But if he shows himself to be to us God, even the Mighty God, we may rely on him with safety. It is good for us that he is called strong or mighty because our contest is with the devil, death, and sin (see Eph. 6:12), enemies too powerful and strong, by whom we would be vanquished immediately if Christ's strength had not made us invincible. Thus we learn from this title that there is in Christ abundance of protection for defending our salvation, so that we desire nothing beyond him; he is God, who is pleased to show himself strong on our behalf. This application may be regarded as the key to this and similar passages, leading us to distinguish between Christ's mysterious essence and the power by which he has revealed himself to us.

The name "Father" is used to mean "author" because Christ preserves the existence of his church through all ages and bestows immortality on the body and on the individual members. We ought, therefore, to elevate our minds to that blessed and everlasting life that as yet we do not see but that we possess by hope and faith (see Rom. 8:2).

If he shows himself to be to us God, even the Mighty God, we may rely on him with safety.

Prince of Peace. This is the last title, and by it the prophet declares that the coming of Christ will be the cause of full and perfect happiness, or at least of calm and blessed safety. The Hebrew word for peace often signifies prosperity, for of all blessings none is better or more desirable than peace. The general meaning is that all who submit to Christ's dominion will lead a quiet and blessed life in obedience to him. Hence it follows that life without this King is restless and miserable.

But we must also take into consideration the nature of this peace. It is the same as that of the kingdom, for it resides chiefly in the conscience; otherwise we must be engaged in incessant conflict and liable to daily attacks. Not only, therefore, does he promise outward peace but that peace by which we who were God's enemies return to a state of favor with him. Justified by faith, says Paul, we have peace with God (see Rom. 5:1).

Of the increase of his government and peace there will be no end. Isaiah begins to explain and confirm what he said before (Christ is the Prince of Peace) by saying that his government extends to every age and is perpetual; there will be no end to the government or to peace. This was also repeated by Daniel, who prophesies that

Christ's kingdom is an everlasting kingdom (see Dan. 7:27). Gabriel also alluded to this when he carried the message to the virgin Mary; and he gave the true exposition of this passage, for it cannot be understood to refer to anyone but Christ. He shall reign, says the angel, over the house of Jacob forever, and of his kingdom there shall be no end (see Luke 1:33). We see that the mightiest governments of this world are unexpectedly overturned and suddenly fall, as if they had been built on a slippery foundation.

To government he adds the eternity of peace, for one cannot be separated from the other. It is impossible for Christ to be King without also keeping his people in calm and blessed peace and enriching them with every blessing. But since they are exposed to innumerable attacks every day and are tossed and perplexed by fears and anxieties, they ought to cultivate that peace of Christ (see Phil. 4:7), so that they might retain their composure amid the destruction of the whole world.

He will reign on David's throne and over his kingdom. David was promised that the Redeemer would spring from his seed (2 Sam. 7:12–13); his kingdom was nothing but an image or faint shadow of that more perfect and truly blessed state that God has determined to establish by the hand of his Son. The prophets remind the people of that remarkable miracle by calling Christ the Branch of David (Jer. 33:15).

When Isaiah writes, "Establishing and upholding it with justice and righteousness from that time on and forever," the words justice and righteousness do not here refer to outward affairs of state. We must observe the analogy between the kingdom of Christ and its qualities; being spiritual, it is established by the power of the Holy Spirit. In a word, all these things must be viewed as referring to the inner person—that is, when we are regenerated by God to true righteousness. It is true that outward righteousness follows, but it must be preceded by the renewal of mind and heart. We are not Christ's, therefore, unless we follow what is good and just and bear on our hearts the stamp of that righteousness that has been sealed by the Holy Spirit.

Excerpted from *Isaiah* by John Calvin. Copyright © 2000 by Watermark, The Crossway Classic Commentaries, edited by Alister McGrath and J. I. Packer. Used by permission of Crossway Books.

13

Wrapped in Humility

ALISTAIR BEGG

"Have this mind among yourselves, which is yours in Christ Jesus, who, though he was in the form of God, did not count equality with God a thing to be grasped, but made himself nothing, taking the form of a servant, being born in the likeness of men."

Philippians 2:5–7

When we look into the night sky along with the shepherds, we see a host of angels. The shepherds are going through their normal duties of keeping sheep when suddenly the sky is filled with splendor and magnificence and song. Inevitably, this surprised them.

But in light of where this child came from, the real surprise is not in the presence of an angelic throng; the real surprise would be the absence of an angelic throng. What would be surprising is if God could come in a moment in time, and do so in a way that wasn't accompanied in some measure by the splendor that had marked him in eternity.

In eternity, the Father, the Son, and the Spirit shared coequally in all God is. The Son who was about to become incarnate was possessed of the glory of God, the likeness of God, the image of God, the splendor of God, indeed, everything that makes God God. Everything that caused the angels to adore God was there in the Lord Jesus Christ. When we begin there, the impact of what follows is staggering.

Sometimes you may hear of someone who is doing something of exceptional worth or kindness, and someone else says about the person, "I'll tell you what's remarkable about her. If you knew where she came from, the fact that she comes down here to do what she's doing is really amazing." They're saying that while what she is doing is significant, if you knew her background, where she came from, and what she left behind, you'd understand that it is all the more remarkable she is here.

The hymn writer of the Christmas carol captures it in two lines:

> Thus to come from highest bliss
> Down to such a world as this.[1]

The Holy Spirit wants us to understand where Christ came from. Paul tells us in Philippians 2:5–7, "Christ Jesus, who, though he was in the form of God, did not count equality with God a thing to be grasped, but made himself nothing, taking the form of a servant, being born in the likeness of men."

Coming in the very form or nature of God, Jesus didn't consider equality with God something to be grasped. In other words, instead of holding on to his own uninterrupted glory, he chose to set it aside.

Paul tells us that "he made himself nothing," or literally, "himself he emptied." In the King James Version we read he, "made himself of no reputation." What does this say?

It says that coming into the world, Christ chose not to arrive in a fashion that was so marked with dignity and style that it would immediately cause people to say, "Oh, this must be God Incarnate."

In fact, remember what the angel said to the shepherds: "This will be a sign to you. You will find the babe, wrapped in swaddling clothes, lying in a manger." What a strange site. Not that the shepherds were unfamiliar with a manger. It was part of their routine activities. But a child in a manger? What child is this that would be laid in a manger? The sign is not a chariot parked outside. It's not a scepter, but a stable.

He "made himself nothing, taking the form of a servant." In other words, he became as much of an earthly servant as he had been a heavenly sovereign.

We see this same picture in another scene much later in Jesus' life:

> Jesus, knowing that the Father had given all things into his hands, and that he had come from God and was going back to God, rose from supper. He laid aside his outer garments, and taking a towel, tied it around his waist. Then he poured water into a basin and began to wash the disciples' feet and to wipe them with the towel that was wrapped around him. (John 13:3–5)

Wrapped in swaddling clothes and lying in a manger . . . wrapped in a towel and wiping his disciples' feet. Taking the form of a servant.

If you look again at Philippians 2:7, you notice that there is a comma after "nothing," and then you have a verb in the present continuous: he "made himself nothing, taking. . . ." There is a link here between nothing and taking.

Alec Motyer, a wonderful scholar and friend of mine, suggests that if we ask, what did he empty himself into? rather than, of what did he empty himself? we will be closer to coming to grips with it.

It's a fantastic paradox. It's what the Lord Jesus took to himself that humbled him, not what he laid aside. He emptied himself, "taking the form of a servant, *being born in the likeness of men.*" It was in taking to himself humanity that he became nothing.

Christ chose not to arrive in a fashion that was so marked with dignity and style that it would immediately cause people to say, "Oh, this must be God Incarnate."

Of course, for those of us who think that man is the apex of it all, we can't imagine anyone who wouldn't be absolutely excited to be a man. But if you were God? Imagine. To be God and come down a birth canal, to be laid in a manger, to live as an outcast, to die as a stranger, to bear the abuse and the curse of the law—it sounds like "nothing" to me.

There's no analogy that is adequate to express this, but it doesn't stop me from trying. Those of you who follow professional golf will know that Andrew Martinez has been a caddy on the PGA tour for a long time for many champion golfers.

Andrew is well known among his friends. He's intelligent and athletic. He is, in his own right, a good golfer; he's a better tennis player; and he's an even better backgammon player. Andrew as Andrew is a somebody in his own right.

But on the occasions that I've been with Andrew when he has made the transition from Andrew, friend and companion, to Andrew, caddy, he's gotten out of the car and walked into the clubhouse and reappeared in white overalls. He has poured himself into something. He has emptied himself by taking. He's still Andrew—athletic, golfer, intelligent. He's still Andrew in all of his essence as Andrew, but by taking to himself, he has emptied himself.

It is not by a diminution that he makes himself nothing. It is by an addition that he makes himself nothing. He has not ceased to be who he is. But by wearing the overalls—by pouring himself into them—he constitutes a completely different entity. He who is a somebody in his own right has become a nobody in order that he might serve others.

Jesus did not approach the incarnation asking, "What's in it for me, what do I get out of it?"

In coming to earth he said, "I don't matter."

Jesus, you're going to be laid in a manger.

"It doesn't matter."

Jesus, you will have nowhere to lay your head.

"It doesn't matter."

Jesus, you will be an outcast and a stranger.

"It doesn't matter."

Jesus, they will nail you to a cross and your followers will all desert you.

And Jesus says, "That's okay."

This is what it means. He "made himself nothing, taking on the form of a servant, being born in the likeness of men."

Adapted from "He Humbled Himself," sermon by Alistair Begg, Parkside Church, Chagrin Falls, Ohio, December 19, 2004. Used by permission.

Scripture quotations are from the English Standard Version.

14

Shepherd Status

RANDY ALCORN

"And in the same region there were shepherds out in the field, keeping watch over their flock by night. And an angel of the Lord appeared to them, and the glory of the Lord shone around them, and they were filled with fear."

Luke 2:8–9

N o Christmas program is complete without its little band of gunnysack shepherds. Frightened by the angel's sudden appearance, they marvel at the good news from the angel and rush to Bethlehem to see the Savior-King. As they return to their flocks, they praise God and tell all who will listen about the birth of the chosen Child.

They finish spreading the good tidings, leave the stage, and we hardly give them another thought.

But why did the announcement come to them at all? Why not to priests and kings? Who were they that they should be eyewitnesses of God's glory and receive history's greatest birth announcement?

In Christ's day, shepherds stood on the bottom rung of the Palestinian social ladder. They shared the same unenviable status as tax collectors and dung sweepers. Only Luke mentions them.

During the time of the patriarchs, shepherding was a noble occupation. Shepherds are mentioned early, in Genesis 4:20, where Jabal is called the father of those living in tents and raising livestock. In nomadic societies, everyone—whether sheikh or slave—was a shepherd. The wealthy sons of Isaac and Jacob tended flocks (Gen. 30:29; 37:12). Jethro, the priest of Midian, employed his daughters as shepherdesses (Ex. 2:16).

When the twelve tribes of Israel migrated to Egypt, they encountered a lifestyle foreign to them. The Egyptians were agriculturalists. As farmers, they despised shepherding because sheep and goats meant death to crops. Battles between farmers and shepherds are as old as they are fierce. The first murder in history erupted from a farmer's resentment of a shepherd (Gen. 4:1–8).

Egyptians considered sheep worthless for food and sacrifice. Egyptian art forms and historical records portray shepherds negatively. Neighboring Arabs—their enemy—were shepherds, and Egyptian hatred climaxed when shepherd kings seized Lower Egypt.

Pharaoh's clean-shaven court looked down on the rugged shepherd sons of Jacob. Joseph matter-of-factly informed his brothers, "All shepherds are detestable to the Egyptians" (Gen. 46:34, NIV).

In the course of four hundred years, the Egyptians prejudiced the Israelites' attitude toward shepherding. Jacob's descendants became accustomed to a settled lifestyle and forgot their nomadic roots. When Israel later settled in Canaan (c. 1400 B.C.), the few tribes still retaining a fondness for pastoral life chose to live in the Transjordan (Num. 32:1–42).

After the settling in Palestine, shepherding ceased to hold its prominent position. As the Israelites acquired more farmland, pasturing decreased. Shepherding became a menial vocation for the laboring class.

Around 1000 BC, David's emergence as king temporarily raised the shepherd's image. The lowliness of this trade made David's promotion striking (2 Sam. 7:8). While poetic sections of Scripture record positive allusions to shepherding, scholars believe these references reflect a literary ideal, not reality.

In the days of the prophets, sheepherders symbolized judgment and social desolation (Zeph. 2:6). Amos contrasted his high calling as prophet with his former role as a shepherd (Amos 7:14). Dr. Joachim Jeremias says shepherds were "despised in everyday life."[1] In general, they were considered second-class and untrustworthy.

Shepherding had not just lost its widespread appeal; it eventually forfeited its social acceptability. Some shepherds earned their poor reputations, but others became victims of a cruel stereotype. The religious leaders maligned the shepherd's good name; rabbis banned pasturing sheep and goats in Israel, except on desert plains.

The Mishnah, Judaism's written record of the oral law, also reflects this prejudice, referring to shepherds in belittling terms. One passage describes them as "incompetent"; another says no one should ever feel obligated to rescue a shepherd who has fallen into a pit.

Jeremias documents the fact that shepherds were deprived of all civil rights. They could not fulfill judicial offices or be admitted in court as witnesses. He writes, "To buy wool, milk, or a kid from a shepherd was forbidden on the assumption that it would be stolen property."[2]

Jeremias notes, "The Rabb. [Rabbis] ask with amazement how, in view of the despicable nature of shepherds, one is to explain the fact that God is called 'my shepherd' in Ps. 23:1."[3]

Smug religious leaders maintained a strict caste system at the expense of shepherds and other common folk. Shepherds were officially labeled "sinners"—a technical term for a class of despised people.

Into this social context of religious snobbery and class prejudice, God's Son stepped forth. How surprising and significant that Father God handpicked lowly, unpretentious shepherds to first hear the joyous news: "It's a boy, and he's Messiah!"

How surprising and significant that Father God handpicked lowly, unpretentious shepherds to first hear the joyous news: "It's a boy, and he's Messiah!"

What an affront to the religious leaders who were so conspicuously absent from the divine mailing list. Even from birth, Christ moved among the lowly. It was the sinners, not the self-righteous, he came to save (Mark 2:17).

The proud religionists of Christ's day have faded into obscurity, but the shepherd figure is once again elevated in church life as pastors "shepherd their flocks." That figure was immortalized by the Lord Jesus when he said, "I am the good shepherd. The good shepherd lays down his life for the sheep" (John 10:11). Christ is also the Great Shepherd (Heb. 13:20) and the Chief Shepherd (1 Pet. 5:4). No other illustration so vividly portrays his tender care and guiding hand.

As we gaze on nativity scenes and smile at those gunnysack shepherds, let's not lose sight of the striking irony. A handful of shepherds, marginalized by the social and religious elite, were chosen to break the silence of centuries, heralding Messiah's birth.

Originally published as "A Second Glance at the Shepherds" by Randy Alcorn, in *Moody Monthly* magazine, December 1982. Used by permission of the author.

Scripture quotations are from the New International Version.

15

Glory Revealed

JOHN MACARTHUR

"And the glory of the LORD shall be revealed."

Isaiah 40:5

"And an angel of the Lord appeared to them,
and the glory of the Lord shone around them. . . ."

Luke 2:9

"He is the radiance of the glory of God."

Hebrews 1:3

The whole concept of the glory of the Lord surrounds the Christmas scene. At the birth of Christ, the Bible says that angels required such a focus as they shouted, "Glory to God in the highest." And Luke 2:9 says, "The glory of the Lord shone around them, and they were greatly afraid" (NKJV). So the glory of the Lord was the angelic focus at the birth of Christ. The glory of the Lord was the aura that invaded the scene. It isn't imposed upon the Christmas story, it *is* the Christmas story.

The word of Isaiah 40:5, "the glory of the LORD shall be revealed" (NKJV), is in fact the Christmas story. It is the Christmas message. The birth of Christ was the revelation of the glory of the Lord . . . just as Isaiah had promised.

"The glory of the Lord shall be revealed." What does that mean? What is the truth bound up in the message of the Spirit of God here?

To begin with, "the glory of the Lord" is the expression of God's person. It is any manifestation of God's character or attributes. In other words, glory is to God what brightness is to the sun. Glory is to God what wet is to water. His glory is like the heat of a fire. In other words, it is the emanation, it is the effulgence, it is the brightness, it is the product of his presence, it is the revelation of himself. Anytime God discloses himself, he manifests his glory.

How could we ever know him if impersonal manifestations of the glory were all we had access to? Therefore Isaiah made this prophecy: "The glory of the Lord shall be revealed."

The heavens declare the glory of God. The beast of the field gives him glory. Everything he ever made shows his glory in some way or another. Everything he ever does speaks of his essence—so that the whole of all created things and all things in existence are revelations of God's glory. They are disclosures of his person. You see his glory in the smallest flower. You see his glory in the butterfly. You see his glory in a tree. You see his glory in the sky. His glory may be seen in everything.

God not only revealed his glory in creation, but God also revealed his glory in a very particular way through the ineffable *shekinah*. This was a physical manifestation of divine glory that appeared to the Israelites of Moses' day as a pillar of light by night and a pillar of cloud by day. This visible expression of the divine presence remained with them as a perpetual reminder of God's deliverance and his care for them, even as they wandered for forty years under his frown because of their disobedience.

Now, I grant you that all the appearances of God's glory have about them a certain air of mystery. No matter how many times you go over it and how many times you think it through, there is connected with the glory of God a kind of marvelous mystery—a cloud, a pillar of fire, blazing light.

If all we had were the creation and the *shekinah*, our understanding of God's glory would be shrouded in confusion. And yet God wants us to know him, and he wants us to perceive him, and he wants us to understand his self-revelation. How could we ever know him if impersonal manifestations of the glory were all we had access to?

Therefore Isaiah made this prophecy: "The glory of the Lord shall be *revealed*." There's coming a greater disclosure, a fuller revelation. Let's see how the New Testament speaks of its fulfillment in Hebrews 1. This is another text that deals with the true Christmas story: "God, who at various times and in various ways spoke in time past to the fathers by the prophets" (Heb. 1:1).

Notice: "God . . . spoke." That's the subject and the verb. The text is speaking about God's self-disclosure. He revealed himself at different times and in different ways.

God had never been silent. After Adam sinned, he and Eve were driven from the garden and the earth was cursed. But God did not remain hidden from Adam's progeny. He did not leave himself shrouded in clouds of darkness. He shone the light of glory—in creation and through the *shekinah*.

But he also spoke through his Word, given to the prophets and recorded in Scripture. He thus disclosed his glory in a way that communicated truth and gave instruction to his people. This was the highest and most enduring manifestation of divine glory Old Testament saints had access to.

You see, God only whispers in his creation. He revealed a shadow of his glory in the *shekinah*. But he speaks with absolute clarity in his Word. "God . . . spoke" (Heb. 1:1)—and not in a whisper but in full voice.

Still, there was an incompleteness in it all until, "[God] has in these last days spoken to us by his Son" (Heb. 1:2).

Now that is God shouting. You can't mistake it. Christ is God, and you see every attribute of God manifest in him: his judgment, his justice, his love, his wisdom, his power, his omniscience. It's all there in person as we see him walk through the world, working his work, living his life. The fullness of God may be seen as it was never seen before in Jesus Christ.

The writer of Hebrews continues in verse 3: "being the brightness of His glory." Who is Jesus Christ? He is the glory of the Lord. That is what he's saying here. Jesus is the "express image" of God (v. 3). He is the personal embodiment of the brightness of God's glory. That's why it says in John 1:14, "The Word became flesh and dwelt among us, and we beheld His glory, the glory as of the only begotten of the Father. . . ."

The phrase "being the brightness of His glory" is very simple. The word "brightness" is *apaugasma*. It means "radiance." It means "to send forth light" or "to send forth brightness." It's simply saying Christ is the shining forth of God. Just as the radiance of the Sun reaches the earth to light us, to warm us, to give us life and growth, so in Christ do we sense the warmth and radiance of the glorious light of God touching the hearts of men. The brightness of the sun is of the same nature as the sun. It is as old as the sun, and never was the sun without its brightness. The brightness of the sun cannot be separated from the sun and yet it is distinct. And so, Christ is God and yet distinct. He is God and yet he is the manifestation of God. He is the glory of the Lord who shouts the reality of God, which was only whispered in time past.

Now what am I saying? The prophet said the glory of the Lord shall be revealed. The writer of Hebrews says the Son is the brightness of his glory. The message of Christmas is that God came into the world in all his glory, and what was only a whisper became a shout. And someday in the future, as we read in the book of Revelation, he will come back in his blazing glory, which Jesus called "great glory." When he comes back in second coming glory, the Bible says the shout will be even louder so that every voice in the universe will cry and shout and sing his praises.

He is the glory of the Lord who shouts the reality of God, which was only whispered in time past.

What does this say to us? We discover in 2 Corinthians 3:18: "But we all, with unveiled face, beholding as in a mirror the glory of the Lord, are being transformed into the same image from glory to glory, just as by the Spirit of the Lord." The veil is taken away. The things that were mysterious, troublesome, and confusing have been made clear. We now behold clearly the glory of the Lord. It's Christ. And as we behold him and look at him and gaze on him, we literally become like him.

Every authentic believer in Christ is being brought to spiritual maturity by that very process. We're gazing at his glory and being transformed into his image in the process.

God wants to transform you into his own image from one level of glory to the next. It is staggering for me to perceive that the Lord Jesus Christ is the glory of the Lord revealed *to* us. It is more staggering to grasp that he is the glory of the Lord revealed *for* us. It is most staggering of all to understand that he is the glory of God revealed *in* us. "Christ in you, the hope of glory."

Adapted from "The Glory of the Lord," sermon by John MacArthur, Grace Community Church, Sun Valley, California, December, 2002. Used by permission.

Scripture quotations are from the New King James Version.

16

Good News of Great Joy

RAYMOND C. ORTLUND JR.

"And the angel said to them, 'Fear not, for behold, I bring you good news of great joy that will be for all the people. For unto you is born this day in the city of David a Savior, who is Christ the Lord. And this will be a sign for you: you will find a baby wrapped in swaddling cloths and lying in a manger.' And suddenly there was with the angel a multitude of the heavenly host praising God and saying,
    'Glory to God in the highest,
    and on earth peace among those with whom he is pleased!'"

Luke 2:10–14

People love to celebrate. People love to break from the routine of life and celebrate. All over the world right now lights are strung and special music is being broadcast and trees are decorated and gifts have been lovingly purchased and lavish feasts are being prepared. The curse over C. S. Lewis's land of Narnia was that it was always winter but never Christmas.

What monotony and tedium and bleak weariness! Life must be punctuated with celebration. It's a universal human impulse. And where did this inclination come from? God created us this way. "What is the chief end of man?" the Westminster Catechism asks. "Man's chief end is to glorify God and to enjoy him forever." Now, that is celebrating worthy of the name!

Several years ago I read a story about a parade somewhere oriented around the theme "Louie, Louie"—the old rock and roll song. There was no reason for this parade. The organizer explained that he just felt like hosting a parade, and that song was as good a reason as any. Whether we have a silly reason or a solid reason, we will celebrate, because God made us this way. And we who belong to Jesus have powerful reasons to celebrate. God has come to us. God has shown that this life is not the only life we will ever know, and that this world is not the only reality we will ever experience. God has thrown open the gates of heaven to us through Christ his Son. We have seen the celebration going on within those gates. And that's where we're headed!

God is there in his glory. He drew aside the curtain of the heavens so that the shepherds could see reality— his glory, which is always there but is usually concealed from our view.

God has set before us solid reasons for joyful celebration in the birth of Jesus Christ. Let's look at Luke 2:8–14 to find some.

Reason for joy number 1: God is there in his glory. That night so long ago the shepherds were guarding their sheep for the umpteenth night in a row. Their fathers had done the same thing on the same hills for generations. Strictly routine. And then God broke in through his angelic herald! And when he did, verse 9 says that "the glory of the Lord shone around them." God's "glory" is his radiant beauty. And he made his glory visible on this special occasion; it "shone" around them. He drew aside the curtain of the heavens so that the shepherds could see reality—his glory, which is always there but is usually concealed from our view.

The nighttime sky above us is not the absolute limit of reality. Our natural eyes only dimly comprehend the fullness of what is. Our routines are not the whole of what God has for us. When he opened the sky above Bethlehem, a shaft of his glory pierced our darkness. We are not left on our own. God is there. How simple and how infinitely wonderful. I remember hearing Francis Schaeffer pray once. He began by saying, "God, I thank you that you exist." I had never thought of thanking God for that. But how obvious. How joyful that someone as glorious as God is really there.

But to these shepherds, God's glorious immediacy offered no joy. They were terrified. We would have been too. And not merely because we are so small compared with God and so drab compared with his glory. It's our guilty consciences that make God terrifying. Santa Claus we can handle. We line up our kids to be photographed with him. But God? What if he were to make an appearance at the mall? No line would form. We would scatter. God is terrifying to guilty sinners, even though he is in himself gloriously beautiful. But God is pursuing us, even though we avoid him. He himself takes the initiative to break through our terror.

Reason for joy number 2: God is good, and his goodness is of a spreading nature. The angel reassures the shepherds with good news. But not just good news. Good news of joy. But not just good news of joy. Good news of great joy, intense joy, rich, full, and overflowing joy. And when the angel concludes his announcement, a back-up group of thousands of other angels suddenly pours down out of heaven, flooding the earthly sky, praising God. I wonder what it sounded like? We know from Isaiah 6 that the thresholds of the temple doors shook at the voices of the seraphim. Is heavenly worship a kind of happily thunderous explosion? I wonder. But in any case, here's the point. If God were unhappy and frustrated and depressed and cranky, how could you explain the joy of the angels? Actually, we never see God himself here in the text. All we're shown is the periphery of God's presence, his effect upon his angelic servants. He lets us nibble at the edges. He allows us to overhear the sounds of heaven, as the door opens briefly before closing again. But we can see enough to know that his presence is *fullness* of joy.

You know when you walk down the aisle of your grocery store and someone offers you a free sample, just a little taste, and lets you know that there's more where that came from? That's what happened to the shepherds here. God is good, and his goodness is of a spreading nature, spilling out of heaven down into this world, spreading out widely, to all the people, without rank or distinction. Verse 11 rejoices that a Savior has been born for us—not for angels, not for the privileged, not for the worthy, but for us.

Reason for joy number 3: God is relevant. He has given us a Savior. A Savior is what we most need. If I'm not yearning for a Savior, I'm the irrelevant one. The greatest thing God could do for us is to give us a Savior. God himself defines true relevance here, because our basic problem in life is not financial or political or intellectual or psychological. Our basic problem is moral. If God spreads joy wherever he goes, we spread trouble wherever we go. Look at the history of the world. The vast majority of people on the face of this earth just want to be happy. We don't mean any harm. We just want to live our quiet little lives and be left alone. And if nearly everybody feels that way, what's gone wrong? Why is the world in such a mess? You and I are the problem. Our good intentions are not strong enough to control our evil impulses. We need a Savior to rescue us from ourselves. And God, with great understanding and compassion, has given us what we most deeply need—a Savior in Jesus Christ. We who have come into Christ are not always going to be the way we are now. The world is not always going to be the way it is now. The Savior has come. Evil is doomed. Our best days still lie ahead.

Reason for joy number 4: God will make sure that he is supremely glorified. "Glory to God in the highest" is the chorus of the angels broadcast into this world of enslavement to drugs and cynical lies and broken dreams and national disgrace. "Glory to God in the highest" proclaims that there is something higher than the height of our sin. God reigns supreme over all, and God will not allow evil to succeed here in his world. He will get himself glory out of this world. And so he should. If God's heart is attuned to love only what is best, then God loves his own glory above all else. He will share his glory with no one, and that is the most wonderful thing of all about God. He will not unGod himself. What if he did? Where would we be then? He steadily, faithfully guides history and our lives toward a God-glorifying conclusion.

> *Why is the world in such a mess? You and I are the problem. Our good intentions are not strong enough to control our evil impulses. We need a Savior to rescue us from ourselves.*

Isn't it interesting how in Christmas cards and on public displays we often see the words, "Peace on earth, good will toward men"? But how seldom we see the prior words, "Glory to God in the highest"! But there is no peace, there is no good will, unless there is glory to God in the highest first. We forget to put God's glory first. Fortunately, he does not. God will be glorified.

Would you or I have begun this announcement the way the angels did, with glory to God first? Obviously, the angels did not understand the importance of relevance and contextualization and meeting felt needs. They started with God, not with peace on earth! Why? Because the most relevant message to this sin-ruined world was, is, and always will be, "Glory to God in the highest." Our whole problem is our God-neglect. But the best news for sinners like you and me is that, whatever we might do, God is still God, God is glorious, and God's glory is supreme over all other realities. And when his glorious kingdom is finally consummated, then there *will* be perfect peace on earth, good will toward men—which leads us to our next reason.

Reason for joy number 5: God is on our side. "On earth peace to men on whom his favor rests." That word "peace" in verse 14 means not a political peace, not a negotiated settlement, not a well-patrolled neighborhood, not metal detectors in our high schools. The peace God creates nurtures our well-being in the broadest, fullest, most enduring sense. The peace God gives is the direct answer to our most human yearnings. And the vital thing to see is that this peace flows out of "Glory to God in the highest." The Puritan preacher Richard Sibbes put it this way:

> God hath joined these two together as one chief end and good. The one, that he might be glorified. The other, that we might be happy. And both these are attained by honoring and serving him. . . . Thus our happiness and God's chief end agree together. . . . What a sweetness is this in God, that in seeking our own good we would glorify him.[1]

Here today the sweetness of God is visiting us again, as with the shepherds so long ago. He is calling us to receive with thankful joy our Savior. He is calling us to join in the heavenly celebration, that we might be happy as he is glorified.

God has come to us in Christ to bring glory to himself in the highest as he grants us peace here in our lives. What can we do but rejoice?

Adapted from "Luke 2:14 and Reasons for Joy at Christmas," sermon by Raymond C. Ortlund Jr., First Presbyterian Church, Augusta, Georgia, December 24, 1998. Used by permission.

Scripture quotations are from the New International Version.

17

Seeing Jesus with the Shepherds

FRANCIS SCHAEFFER

"And they went with haste and found Mary and Joseph, and the baby lying in a manger. And when they saw it, they made known the saying that had been told them concerning this child. And all who heard it wondered at what the shepherds told them."

Luke 2:16–18

After the angels had appeared to them, the shepherds of Bethlehem ran down the hill to see the baby they had been told about. They came "with haste." Luke's account in Luke 2:8–18 ties together a glorious opening of the heavens, the speaking or singing of angels, and some ordinary shepherds who were simply tending their flocks. The utterly supernatural took place in the framework of their natural habitat, and their reaction was simple and human: "We've heard about this thing; let's go see it." In a profound sense, the act of religious intensity is as natural as any other movement of life. And they went to Bethlehem with haste, obviously because of the reality of the situation that confronted them.

He is here to cut the nerve of man's real dilemma, to solve the problem from which all other problems flow. Man is a sinner who needs an overwhelming love. Jesus has come to save his people from their sins.

Let us imagine that we are with the shepherds on those hills in Palestine. We have seen and heard the angels, and we have begun to run to Bethlehem. We come bursting into the presence of Mary, Joseph, and the baby, and immediately we wonder: what are we looking at?

First of all, we are looking at a true baby. He is not an idea or a religious experience. He is a newborn infant who makes noises and cries when he gets hungry. What we are looking at is real, simple, definite, complete. We are looking at a true baby.

There is no reason to think that the baby shows any special manifestations. An artist such as Rembrandt can paint him with light emanating from his body, and if we understand the light as symbolic, it is safe enough. But if we think of it as more than that, it is harmful. There is no halo about the baby's head. Certainly there is no halo around Mary's head. What we see is a young Jewish mother, probably seventeen or eighteen years old. She may be pretty or she may not be. We see her husband, and we see a little baby who does not show any marks that would distinguish him from any other infant. And yet this little baby we see lying here is the second person of the Trinity. He himself has been God forever. This baby is God who has taken on flesh.

Why did God come into this world? Only the scriptural answer will suffice: the second person of the Trinity has been born because he loves the world.

But why did he come this way, as a little baby? Why did he choose to lie in a manger and be cared for by a human mother, with the sweetness but the utter weakness of a newborn babe? He came this way because he came to meet the central need of men. He did not come to overthrow the Romans, though a lot of the Jews would have loved that. If he had, he would have come riding on a great conquering steed. The central reason he came was not to raise the living standards of the world. Surely if modern man were going to vote on the way he would like a messiah to appear, he would want him loaded down with moneybags from heaven. He did not come primarily to teach and relieve ignorance—perhaps then he would have come laden with books. An angel had revealed to Joseph the primary task for which he came: "Thou shalt call his name JESUS; for he shall save his people from their sins" (Matt. 1:21).

In the light of their experience of looking at the face of the baby Jesus, in the light of their understanding of that situation, can we imagine them continuing to live in sin as though it were normal, without being sorry and having real repentance? I think not.

He is here to cut the nerve of man's real dilemma, to solve the problem from which all other problems flow. Man is a sinner who needs an overwhelming love. Jesus has come to save his people from their sins.

Many believed in him when he was still an infant, and when they did so the baby became their Savior. The shepherds believed, regardless of the simplicity with which they understood: "And the shepherds returned, glorifying and praising God for all the things that they had heard and seen, as it was told unto them" (Luke 2:20). Though they believed with less understanding than we who have the New Testament, and though we might even think of them as believing within the Old Testament framework as Old Testament saints, they nonetheless did believe, and they will be in heaven with us. They are in the church of Jesus Christ.

But many, I am sure, did not believe. The shepherds must have run into a tremendous dilemma when "they made known abroad the saying which was told them concerning this child" (Luke 2:17). Luke goes on to tell us that "all they that heard it wondered at those things which were told them by the shepherds" (Luke 2:18), and we cannot doubt that those who wondered must have been split into two camps. Some believed, while others did not. Some must have shrugged their shoulders: "All right, but I don't need a Savior."

As we ourselves have run down the hill with the shepherds, looked at the baby, and heard the shepherds' testimony, have we believed? If we have, that is a happy thing indeed, for it means we are now Christians. That is fine, but then we must ask ourselves: what difference has this looking made in our present lives?

At Christmastime, we set up our Christmas trees and toy trains. We may even walk along singing carols, or we may preach a sermon, but these bits and pieces are barren if we are thinking only of them or even thinking only of being in heaven, and are not stopping to ask ourselves, "What difference does it make in my life now?"

What difference *has* looking made? I think we can approach the answer by thinking about the shepherds. Having had this overwhelming experience in the midst of their normal environment and having believed in the Savior, can we imagine one of the shepherds remarking, "It's very nice that I've seen an angel, and it is nice I have seen the Christ, the Messiah the Jews have been waiting for, for so long. It's nice that I've believed in him (unlike some of the other people in Bethlehem) and that I'm going to be in heaven. But really, in practice, it's not going to make any difference at all in my life." This is inconceivable.

Since the shepherds were much like each one of us, they faced a round of old sins when they returned to life as usual. In the light of their experience of looking at the face of the baby Jesus, in the light of their understanding of that situation, can we imagine them continuing to live in sin as though it were normal, without being sorry and having real repentance? I think not. I would suggest that the shepherds, full of the reality of what they had seen in the heavens and in the manger, would have been sorry for their past sins and even more if they sinned again.

Having seen the glory of the heavenly host, could a shepherd any longer think of himself as the center of the universe, expecting all things to get out of his way?

We can imagine a shepherd being jeered at by the first man to whom he told his story, but can we imagine the ridicule stopping him? The shepherd might have been brought up short; successive jeers might have worn him down; but surely, because of the objective reality through which he personally had gone, he would not have been silenced.

While the reality of all this was upon the shepherds, I think prayer would have been an exceedingly simple experience. Communication with God would have become easy because they had seen the supernatural. For if the shepherds heard the angels, why shouldn't God now hear the shepherds?

Having seen the glory of the heavenly host, could a shepherd any longer think of himself as the center of the universe, expecting all things to get out of his way? The glory would have been too overwhelming. Facing the glory of heaven, the shepherds of Bethlehem surely would not have thought that they could drive their little cart through all the universe, stamping harshly upon God's place.

Likewise it is difficult to imagine the shepherds quarreling about personal prerogatives. I cannot imagine being faced with the glory of heaven and the Savior of the world and then immediately saying to someone else, "I'm first, fellow. I'm first."

After this experience, would the shepherds have accepted materialism as either an adequate philosophy or an adequate practice in life? Wouldn't looking at the glory of heaven readjust one's values? I think so. Grasping to have gold jingling in the pockets and angels singing in the heavens do not quite fit together.

The angel had said to them, "Fear not: for, behold, I bring you good tidings of great joy, which shall be to all people. For unto you is born this day in the city of David a Savior, which is Christ the Lord" (Luke 2:10–11). Joy is part of this too. Certainly the shepherds were glad.

This does not mean a stupid kind of happiness or a sick smile, nor does it mean there are no tears or that things in this world are not as bad as God says they are. This joy is connected with the reality of our knowledge of who Jesus is, our relationship with him, and our worship of him.

Imagine you are a shepherd on the hillside, and when the heavenly host appears you are not to be afraid; you are to have joy.

It is the same with all the teaching of the gospel that flows from the event when the shepherds saw and heard the angels, when they ran down the hill and looked upon Jesus. This is the difference it makes in our lives. "And they worshiped him . . . with great joy."

Excerpted from *No Little People* by Francis Schaeffer. Copyright © 1974 by L'Abri Fellowship. Used by permission of Crossway Books.

Scripture quotations are from the King James Version.

18

The Lessons of the Wise Men

J. C. RYLE

"Now after Jesus was born in Bethlehem of Judea in the days of Herod the king, behold, wise men from the east came to Jerusalem, saying, 'Where is he who has been born king of the Jews? For we saw his star when it rose and have come to worship him.' When Herod the king heard this, he was troubled, and all Jerusalem with him; and assembling all the chief priests and scribes of the people, he inquired of them where the Christ was to be born. They told him, 'In Bethlehem of Judea, for so it is written by the prophet:

"And you, O Bethlehem, in the land of Judah,
     are by no means least among the rulers of Judah;
for from you shall come a ruler
     who will shepherd my people Israel."'

Then Herod summoned the wise men secretly and ascertained from them what time the star had appeared. And he sent them to Bethlehem, saying, 'Go and search diligently for the child, and when you have found him, bring me word, that I too may come and worship him.' After listening to the king, they went on their way. And behold, the star that they had seen when it rose went before them until it came to rest over the place where the child was. When they saw the star, they rejoiced exceedingly with great joy. And going into the house they saw the child with Mary his mother, and they fell down and worshiped him. Then, opening their treasures, they offered him gifts, gold and frankincense and myrrh. And being warned in a dream not to return to Herod, they departed to their own country by another way."

Matthew 2:1–12

I t is not known who these wise men were. Their names and dwelling place are both kept back from us. We are only told that they came "from the east." Whether they were Babylonians or Arabs we cannot say. Whether they learned to expect Christ from the ten tribes who went into captivity or from the prophecies of Daniel, we do not know. It matters little who they were. The point that concerns us most is the important lesson which their story gives us.

These verses show us that there may be true servants of God in places where we should not expect to find them. The Lord Jesus has many "hidden ones," like these wise men. Their story on earth may be as little known as that of Melchizedek, Jethro, and Job. But their names are in the book of life, and they will be found with Christ on the day of his appearing. It is well to remember this. We must not look round the earth and say hastily, "All is barren." The grace of God is not tied to places and families. The Holy Spirit can lead souls to Christ without the help of any outward means. Men may be born in dark places of the earth, like these wise men, and yet like them be made "wise for salvation." There are some traveling to heaven at this moment, of whom the church and the world know nothing. They flourish in secret places like the "lily among thorns," and seem to "waste their sweetness on the desert air." But Christ loves them, and they love Christ.

Second, these verses show that it is not always those who have most religious privileges who give Christ most honor. We might have thought that the scribes and Pharisees would have been the first to hasten to Bethlehem, on the slightest rumor that the Savior was born. But it was not so. A few unknown strangers from a distant land were the first, except for the shepherds mentioned by St. Luke, to rejoice at his birth. "He came to that which was his own, but his own did not receive him" (John 1:11). What a mournful picture this is of human nature! How often the same kind of thing may be seen among ourselves! How often the very people who live nearest to the means of grace are those who neglect them most! There is only too much truth in the old proverb, "The nearer the church the farther from God." Familiarity with sacred things has an awful tendency to make men despise them. There are many who, from residence and convenience, ought to be first and foremost in the worship of God, and yet are always last. There are many who might well be expected to be last, who are always first.

Third, these verses show us that there may be knowledge of Scripture in the head, while there is no grace in the heart. We are told that King Herod sent to inquire of the priests and elders "where the Christ was to be born" (v. 4). We are told that they gave him a quick answer, and showed an accurate acquaintance with the letter of Scripture. But they never went to Bethlehem to seek the coming Savior. They would not believe in him when he ministered among them. Their heads were better than their hearts. Let us beware of resting satisfied with head knowledge. It is an excellent thing when rightly used. But a person may have much of it, and still perish everlastingly. What is the state of our hearts? This is the great question. A little grace is better than many gifts. Gifts alone save no one; but grace leads on to glory.

Fourth, these verses show us a splendid example of spiritual diligence. What trouble it must have cost these wise men to travel from their homes to the house where Jesus was born! How many weary miles they must have journeyed! The fatigues of an Eastern traveler are far greater than we can at all understand. The time that such a journey would occupy must have been very great. The dangers to be encountered were neither few nor small. But none of these things moved them. They had set their hearts on seeing him "who has been born king of the Jews" (v. 2), and they never rested till they saw him. They prove to us the truth of the old saying, "Where there is a will there is a way."

They saw no miracles to convince them. They heard no teaching to persuade them. They saw nothing but a newborn infant, helpless and weak, needing a mother's care like any of us. And yet when they saw that infant, they believed that they saw the divine Savior of the world!

It would be well for all professing Christians if they were more ready to follow the example of these good men. Where is our self-denial? What pains do we take about means of grace? What diligence do we show about following Christ? What does our religion cost us? These are serious questions. They deserve serious consideration. The truly "wise," it may be feared, are very few.

Fifth, these verses show us a striking example of faith. These wise men believed in Christ when they had never seen him; but that was not all. They believed in him when the scribes and Pharisees were unbelieving; but that again was not all. They believed in him when they saw him as a little infant on Mary's knees, and worshiped him as King. This was the crowning point of their faith. They saw no miracles to convince them. They heard no teaching to persuade them. They saw nothing but a newborn infant, helpless and weak, needing a mother's care like any of us. And yet when they saw that infant, they believed that they saw the divine Savior of the world! "They bowed down and worshiped him" (v. 11).

We read of no greater faith than this in the whole volume of the Bible. It is a faith that deserves to be placed side by side with that of the penitent thief. The thief saw someone dying the death of a criminal, and yet prayed to him, and "called him Lord." The wise men saw a newborn baby on the lap of a poor woman, and yet worshiped him, and confessed that he was Christ. Blessed indeed are those who can believe in this way!

This is the kind of faith that God delights to honor. We see the proof of that to this very day. Wherever the Bible is read, the conduct of these wise men is known and told as a memorial to them. Let us walk in the steps of their faith. Let us not be ashamed to believe in Jesus and confess him, though all around us remain indifferent and unbelieving. Have we not a thousand times more evidence than the wise men had, to make us believe that Jesus is the Christ?

Excerpted from *Matthew (Expository Thoughts on the Gospels)* by J. C. Ryle. Copyright © 1993 by Watermark. Used by permission of Crossway Books.

Scripture quotations are from the New International Version.

19

Gifts of Faith

JAMES MONTGOMERY BOICE

"Now after Jesus was born in Bethlehem of Judea in the days of Herod the king, behold, wise men from the east came to Jerusalem, saying, 'Where is he who has been born king of the Jews? For we saw his star when it rose and have come to worship him. . . .'

And going into the house they saw the child with Mary his mother, and they fell down and worshiped him. Then, opening their treasures, they offered him gifts, gold and frankincense and myrrh."

Matthew 2:1–2, 11

In Matthew we are told that some time after the birth of Jesus Christ—perhaps as much as two years after the event—wise men from the East came to worship him. This simple story has always figured largely in most celebrations of Christmas, in this and other countries. Because it is an event upon which the imagination may easily take hold, it has been embellished widely both in literature and art.

From the Bible story we know very little about the wise men. Millions of Christmas cards show three kings presenting gifts to a tiny child in a manger. People sing "We Three Kings of Orient Are." But we do not know that there were three wise men who brought the gifts. We are not told that they were kings, or even when they arrived in Bethlehem. It is likely, actually, in view of their long journey and of Herod's command that all children under two years of age be killed, that they arrived when the infant Jesus had already become a young child.

The fact that so little information is given about the wise men clearly shows that Matthew's interest was not focused upon the wise men themselves. Rather, he was interested in the fact that Gentiles came to worship the Jewish Messiah, and in the gifts they bore. A literary critic would draw special attention to the gifts, for they occur at the end of the story after the child has been found and thus occupy a place of prominence.

It is easy to see why gold is an appropriate gift for Jesus Christ. Gold is the metal of kings. When gold was presented to Jesus, it acknowledged his right to rule. It has often been pointed out that when the wise men brought gold to the infant Jesus they were being used by God to provide the funds necessary for Joseph to take the young child and his mother to Egypt to escape Herod's attempt on his life. That is probably true; but although it is true, it is far overshadowed by the significance of the gift itself. Jesus was a king, as the wise men knew. He was the King of kings. The wise men pointed to his kingship with their gold.

Is it also easy to see why incense was a significant gift. Incense was used in the temple worship. It was mixed with the oil that was used to anoint the priests of Israel. It was part of the meal offerings that were offerings of thanksgiving and praise to God. In presenting this gift the wise men pointed to Christ as our great

High Priest, the one whose whole life was acceptable and well pleasing to his Father.

It is interesting that incense was never mixed with sin offerings. The meat and wine offerings were offerings for sin, and those were not to have incense mixed with them. Only the meal offerings, which were not for sin, were to receive the incense.

When we discover that, we think naturally of Jesus, to whom the incense was given. He was without sin. When his enemies came to him on one occasion, he challenged them with the question, "Can any of you prove me guilty of sin?" (John 8:46). They were speechless.

Just as gold speaks of Christ's kingship and incense speaks of the perfection of his life, so does myrrh speak of his death.

Earlier he had said of his Father, "I always do what pleases him" (John 8:29). None of us can say that. Since only the Lord Jesus Christ was sinless, it was extremely fitting that incense should have been offered to him.

Just as gold speaks of Christ's kingship and incense speaks of the perfection of his life, so does myrrh speak of his death. Myrrh was used in embalming. By any human measure it would be odd, if not offensive, to present to the infant Christ a spice used for embalming. But it was not offensive in this case, nor was it odd. It was a gift of faith. We do not know precisely what the wise men may have known or guessed about Christ's ministry, but we do know that the Old Testament again and again foretold his suffering. Psalm 22 describes his death by crucifixion; it was a verse from this psalm that Jesus quoted when he cried out from the cross, "My God, my God, why have you forsaken me?" (Ps. 22:1; Matt. 27:46).

Isaiah 53:4–5 says, "Surely he took up our infirmities and carried our sorrows, yet we considered him stricken by God, smitten by him, and afflicted. But he was pierced for our transgressions, he was crushed for our iniquities; the punishment that brought us peace was upon him, and by his wounds we are healed." Christ was to suffer, to die for sin. It was myrrh that symbolized this aspect of his ministry.

There were a few other uses of myrrh in the ancient world, one of which is particularly important here. In Mark 15:23 we read that, when Jesus was crucified, the soldiers who performed the crucifixion offered him wine mixed with myrrh and that he did not receive it. In John 19:30 we are told that later when some wine was again offered to him he did receive it. What was the difference? The difference was that in the first case myrrh, which helped to deaden pain, was mixed with the wine. Since Jesus wished to bear all that suffering and death could bring to him, when he had tasted the myrrh he turned away. Later, in order to fulfill Psalm 69:21, which says, "They . . . gave me vinegar for my thirst," he called for something and drank what was offered. Myrrh was used to deaden pain. Jesus wished to suffer all that accompanied death when he died for us.

There is a sense in which by faith we too may present our gifts of gold, incense, and myrrh.

Begin with your myrrh. Myrrh is not only a symbol of Christ's death but also of the spiritual death that should come to you for your sin. Lay it at Christ's feet, saying, "Lord Jesus Christ, I know that I am less perfect than you are and am a sinner. I know that I should receive the consequence of my sin, which is to be barred from your presence forever. But you took my sin, dying in my place. I believe that. Now I ask you to accept me as your child forever."

After you have done that, come with your incense, acknowledging that your life is as impure as the life of the Lord Jesus Christ is sinless. The Bible teaches that there is no good in man that is not mixed with evil. But it also teaches that Christ comes to live in the believer so that the good deeds produced in his or her life may become in their turn "a fragrant offering, an acceptable sacrifice, pleasing to God."

Finally, come with your gold. Gold symbolizes royalty. So when you come with your gold you acknowledge the right of Christ to rule your life. You say, "I am your servant; you are my Master. Direct my life and lead me in it so that I might grow up spiritually to honor and to serve you accordingly."

If you have come believing in all that the myrrh, incense, and gold signify, you have embarked on a path of great spiritual joy and blessing. For those are the gifts of faith. They are the only things we can offer to the one who by grace has given all things to us.

Excerpted from *The Christ of Christmas* by James Montgomery Boice, Moody Press, 1983. Used by permission of Linda Boice.

Scripture quotations are from the New International Version.

20

Embarking on a Course
of Redemption

R. C. SPROUL

"And at the end of eight days, when he was circumcised, he was called Jesus, the name given by the angel before he was conceived in the womb."

Luke 2:21

Eight days after the wondrous birth of Jesus his parents had him circumcised according to the regulations established in Jewish law. This was done in accord with the Law of Moses in the Old Testament (Lev. 12:1–8). The rite of circumcision had been instituted by God as an outward sign of his covenant with Abraham. The word *covenant* indicates an agreement or contract between two or more parties.

A vital part of the covenant was its ratification. The ratification usually involved a rite of blood. The Hebrew word for "covenant" is *berith*. This term originally meant a "cutting." This is important because in ancient Israel a covenant treaty was not merely written but was cut in blood. The covenant with Moses was ratified in blood. The original cutting rite that ratified God's covenant with Abraham was the cutting rite of circumcision.

Circumcision is both the sign of the blessing and of the curse. It signifies the promise of blessing in that as the foreskin is cut off or separated from the body, so Israel is separated out from or consecrated to the Lord. The descendants of Abraham are promised a special blessing if they keep faith with the covenant. The special privileges or blessings are marked in the flesh of those circumcised. At the same time the circumcised flesh is a perpetual reminder of the curse that will fall upon those who disobey the stipulations. The penalty for failure to circumcise the male child was to be "cut off from his people." One was either circumcised unto God or circumcised apart from God and the nation.

When Jesus dies on the cross, he takes upon himself the full curse due to his people. The cross is the ultimate rite of circumcision.

As a sign of the curse of the covenant, circumcision symbolized this idea: "If I fail to keep the terms of the covenant I will be cut off from God and all his benefits even as the foreskin of my flesh has been cut off."

The dramatic symbolism of this rite finds its highest expression in the crucifixion of Christ. When Jesus dies on the cross, he takes upon himself the full curse due to his people. The cross is the ultimate rite of circumcision.

When Jesus is presented by his parents for circumcision, we see his submission to the Law of the covenant. Jesus now becomes an heir to the covenant of Israel. That the sanctions of the covenant are imposed upon the Son of God indicates both his humiliation and his glory. He now enters his role as the New Adam, the author of a glorified humanity. He is the one destined to fulfill the Law in every detail and to win the blessings of the covenant for his people.

EMBARKING ON A COURSE OF REDEMPTION

Where we fail and become covenant-breakers, deserving the curse of the covenant, Jesus, our champion, succeeds in his role as the New Adam, the supreme covenant-keeper.

We are not merely redeemed by the death of Christ; we are also redeemed by the life of Christ. His death on the cross reveals the nadir of his humiliation as he bears the curse for us. But that is only part of his redemptive achievement. It is not enough for us merely to have our sins atoned for. To receive the blessing of the covenant we must possess real righteousness. We need what we cannot supply for ourselves. This merit of righteousness is earned for us by Jesus' life of perfect obedience.

The act of divine creation demonstrates the power to bring something out of nothing. The conception of a baby in the womb of Mary is a divine act of creation ex nihilo, out of nothing. It is a work that only God can perform.

We see then that by undergoing circumcision Jesus is not merely part of a meaningless ritual; he is embarking on a course of redemption as the New Adam.

At the time Jesus is presented for circumcision he also received his name: "And at the end of eight days, when he was circumcised, he was called Jesus, the name given by the angel before he was conceived in the womb" (Luke 2:21).

Jesus did not receive his name from Mary and Joseph. It was customary for the parents of a child to bestow the child's name upon him. But in the case of Jesus his name was mandated by the angel:

> But as he considered these things, behold, an angel of the Lord appeared to him in a dream, saying, "Joseph, son of David, do not fear to take Mary as your wife, for that which is conceived in her is from the Holy Spirit. She will bear a son, and you shall call his name Jesus, for he will save his people from their sins." (Matt. 1:20–21)

The reason given by the angel for the name of Jesus is twofold. In the first instance it is because of the unique circumstances of Jesus' conception and birth. Jesus is uniquely the Son of God. He is the *monogene*, the "only begotten" of the Father (John 1:14). His conception differs from that of any other child. He is conceived not by the ordinary means of human generation, but by the power of the Holy Spirit.

The conception of Jesus calls attention to the glory that surrounds his birth. The virgin birth is not explained in detail by the New Testament. We are told simply that the Holy Spirit would come upon Mary and "overshadow" her. This overshadowing is not elucidated in terms of biology. It is reminiscent, however, of the divine power and method of creation itself. The act of divine creation demonstrates the power to bring something out of nothing. The conception of a baby in the womb of Mary is a divine act of creation *ex nihilo*, out of nothing. It is a work that only God can perform. The normal process of union of sperms and ovum is bypassed. This child is conceived by the power of the Holy Spirit.

We are reminded here of the Genesis account of creation. We read in the biblical narrative this description of the original creation: "The earth was without form and void, and darkness was over the face of the deep. And the Spirit of God was hovering over the face of the waters" (Gen. 1:2). The hovering of the Spirit over the deep was the pulsating beginning of the universe. As the Holy Spirit overshadowed the deep and brought forth a created universe, so the same Spirit overshadowed a peasant virgin to conceive the Son of God.

The second significance of the name of Jesus goes beyond the matter of the source of his life and touches upon the purpose of it. His name is given by God to indicate his divine vocation. He is called "Jesus"—the name means "God saves"—because his task is to save his people from their sin. Though Jesus' birth was attended by humiliation, especially in his subjection to the stipulations of the covenant and his exposure to the curse of the Law, his birth is not without elements of glory. His conception was in glory, and his vocation indicated by his name was a glorious vocation.

21

Those to Whom Christ Comes

R. KENT HUGHES

"And when the time came for their purification according to the Law of Moses, they brought him up to Jerusalem to present him to the Lord (as it is written in the Law of the Lord, 'Every male who first opens the womb shall be called holy to the Lord') and to offer a sacrifice according to what is said in the Law of the Lord, 'a pair of turtledoves, or two young pigeons.' Now there was a man in Jerusalem, whose name was Simeon, and this man was righteous and devout, waiting for the consolation of Israel, and the Holy Spirit was upon him. And it had been revealed to him by the Holy Spirit that he would not see death before he had seen the Lord's Christ. And he came in the Spirit into the temple, and when the parents brought in the child Jesus, to do for him according to the custom of the Law, he took him up in his arms and blessed God and said,

 'Lord, now you are letting your servant depart in peace,
  according to your word;
 for my eyes have seen your salvation
  that you have prepared in the presence of all peoples,
 a light for revelation to the Gentiles,
  and for glory to your people Israel.'

And his father and his mother marveled at what was said about him. And Simeon blessed them and said to Mary his mother, 'Behold, this child is appointed for the fall and rising of many in Israel, and for a sign that is opposed (and a sword will pierce through your own soul also), so that thoughts from many hearts may be revealed.'

And there was a prophetess, Anna, the daughter of Phanuel, of the tribe of Asher. She was advanced in years, having lived with her husband seven years from when she was a virgin, and then as a widow until she was eighty-four. She did not depart from the temple, worshiping with fasting and prayer night and day. And coming up at that very hour she began to give thanks to God and to speak of him to all who were waiting for the redemption of Jerusalem."

Luke 2:22–38

The poverty of Jesus' parents was obvious, considering the humble offering they made for Mary's purification in obedience to the Law. Christianity began and always begins with a spirit of need—spiritual destitution. This was the persistent refrain of Christ's life. We heard it in Mary's *Magnificat*: "for he has been mindful of the humble state of his servant" (1:48). The angels' revelation to the outcast shepherds, rather than to the high and mighty of Israel, sang this as well.

God did not and does not come to the self-sufficient. Christianity wrongly understood gives some an illusive sense of personal spiritual adequacy. Even the born again can wrongly turn spiritual advance into prideful self-sufficiency—a sense that one has arrived. We must continually guard against this within ourselves. Our only adequacy is in Christ (cf. 2 Cor. 3:5)!

While Mary and Joseph were in the temple, they met two other Israelites whose lives exemplified godliness and faith.

Simeon and Anna embodied all that was good in Israelite piety. Both were filled with expectancy. Simeon is described as a man "waiting for the consolation of Israel" (Luke 2:25). The word used here for "consolation" appears in verbal forms in the Greek Old Testament translation of Isaiah in verses that refer to the Messiah, such as 40:1, "Comfort, comfort my people," and 66:13, "As a mother comforts her child, so will I comfort you; and you will be comforted over Jerusalem." Messianic expectation had impacted the lives of Simeon and Anna, and they shared the same electric joy. Anna joined Simeon right after his prophetic song and "spoke about the child to all who were looking forward to the redemption of Jerusalem" (Luke 2:38). Anna was Simeon's co-celebrant of the consolation of Israel. They *believed* when few others truly believed in Christ's coming. They never gave up but kept trusting and looking. What an example they are even for us today!

Simeon and Anna represented all who saw that their only hope was in the mercy and grace of God. Along with the poor carpenter and his wife and the outcast shepherds, they were flesh-and-blood examples of those to whom Christ comes. They personified the paradox of being profoundly empty and profoundly full—"Blessed are those who hunger and thirst for righteousness, for they will be filled" (Matt. 5:6). They longed for the righteousness and consolations that would come only through the Messiah. They came to God's house hungry, and they received as few others have in the history of the world.

Lives like these are rare. Such longing is not in vogue today. The ideal twentieth-century man sees himself as fulfilling Hemingway's line, "You're the completest man I've ever known." He needs nothing, no one, not even God—or so he thinks. We need to ask God to show us our insufficiency. What grace would come to us if we dared to pray for a greater sense of our spiritual need!

There is yet another facet to Simeon's beautiful soul. "It had been revealed to him by the Holy Spirit that he would not die before he had seen the Lord's Christ" (Luke 2:26). Simeon had received an oracle from God, making it clear that though he was aged, he would not leave this life without seeing the Lord's Messiah. How long had he been waiting? Days—months—years? We do not know. But we can imagine his settled assurance and joyous anticipation as he daily came to the temple looking, reflecting, and sometimes asking himself, "Is this the One? There is a likely couple! Maybe this is him!" And then, one grand day, "moved by the Spirit, he went into the temple courts. When the parents brought in the child Jesus to do for him what the custom of the Law required, Simeon took him in his arms and praised God . . ." (vv. 27–28).

With trembling arms Simeon lifted the fat, dimpled baby from the startled virgin, and for a moment the world ceased to turn. The man of God was, as the early church called him, *Theodoches*—God-receiver!

As he held the baby Jesus, he began to praise God in song, and his song laid down for Mary and Joseph (and for us) the purpose of the Christ Child. "Sovereign Lord, as you have promised, you now dismiss your servant in peace" (v. 29).

With the baby in his arms, secure in God's presence, Simeon experienced a profound peace of soul. And well he should have. After all, he held in his hands the "Prince of Peace," the one of whom the angels sang, "Glory to God in the highest, and on earth peace to men on whom his favor rests" (Luke 2:14). God's favor rested upon Simeon. He was ready to die, for that is what "dismiss" means. He was ready to go home to be with his God forever.

Simeon's reason was clear: "For my eyes have seen your salvation" (v. 30). The baby Jesus was and is God's salvation. Moreover, he did not say, "My eyes have seen *part of* your salvation!" Christ is totally sufficient. He is all we need!

True peace comes only when we, like Simeon, understand that salvation is Jesus Christ plus nothing—and rest our souls in him alone.

The salvation of which Simeon sang is universal in its offer—"which you have prepared in the sight of all people, a light for revelation to the Gentiles and for glory to your people Israel" (vv. 31–32). This is especially significant for Gentiles (the majority of the world's population). We were sung about in the Jewish temple by a prophet as he held the Messiah in his arms! Jesus is our "light" in this dark world, he is our salvation, and he is at the same time the "glory [of] . . . Israel." Christ, a light to Gentiles, is the full realization of Israel's glory.

With trembling arms Simeon lifted the fat, dimpled baby from the startled virgin, and for a moment the world ceased to turn. The man of God was, as the early church called him, Theodoches— God-receiver!

Simeon surely held the baby tight. It would have been impossible for him to do otherwise given his ecstasy. He looked at Jesus—and looked—and looked again. His heart, overflowing with joy at the coming of the Redeemer and the fulfillment of God's personal promise to him, soared even beyond his song.

To receive salvation, all one has to do is to take Jesus in his or her arms as Lord. Verse 33 tells us, "The child's father and mother marveled at what was said about him." Surely that amazement impressed every syllable, every instant upon their minds, confirming what had previously been shown to them. May we share their profound amazement and hold every word close to our hearts.

The encounter closes with Simeon turning to Mary and Joseph

and addressing them directly, especially Mary: "Then Simeon blessed them and said to Mary, his mother: 'This child is destined to cause the falling and rising of many in Israel, and to be a sign that will be spoken against, so that the thoughts of many hearts will be revealed. And a sword will pierce your own soul too'" (vv. 34–35). These words are meant for all of us, though the mention of the sword piercing Mary's soul is for her alone.

This prophecy would become very important to Mary. In her *Magnificat* she sang of how the future generations would call her "blessed." But here she learns that the future will also bring great sorrow.

That future would include the family's flight to Egypt, her Son's being misunderstood and rejected, the terrible events of Passion Week, and watching her Son die on the cross.

> Hanging all torn she sees; and in His woes
> And pains; her pangs and throes.[1]

A great sword would go right through this mother's soul! The most honored woman of all would know great pain.

The rest of Simeon's prophetic words apply to all of us. Simeon's assertion that "this child is destined to cause the falling and rising of many" (v. 34a) reveals the necessary experience of all who come to Christ, for we must bow in humiliation and poverty of spirit before we can rise to new life in Christ. When we see our inadequacy, we are ready for God's grace.

Truly Jesus has been "a sign that will be spoken against, so that the thoughts of many hearts will be revealed" (vv. 34b, 35a). When people truly encounter Christ, their inner thoughts (that is, their evil thoughts) are seen for what they are. Apart from God's merciful intervention, people naturally oppose him. But Christ reveals what our inner lives are really like. Human goodness is seen as filthy rags. Unable or unwilling to handle the truth, we naturally oppose Christ's work. But when we fall before him in humiliation, we receive grace and new life. Jesus always knocks us down so he can pick us up.

Excerpted from *Luke: That You May Know the Truth* by R. Kent Hughes. Copyright © 1998 by R. Kent Hughes. Used by permission of Crossway Books.

Scripture quotations are from the New International Version.

22

A Christmas Longing

JONI EARECKSON TADA

"God is the answer to our deepest longings."
1 Corinthians 6:13 (PHILLIPS)

Rummaging through our garage one December afternoon, I sniffed the unmistakable fragrance of new leather. There it was behind a box—a new pony bridle.

From that moment, Santa Claus was dethroned from my childhood. That was it. No more 7-Up and cookies left on the mantelpiece on Christmas Eve. No more bleeding-heart letters to the North Pole. No more sugar for the reindeer. Carrots, either. I was relieved. Something deep down told me it had all been a ploy, anyway. That's when Christmas became more . . . serious. No, not somber. Just more important.

I was only seven years old, but from then on, it was clear that December 25 was a special day. A holy day. The candlelight Christmas Eve service at our Reformed Episcopal church had new and deeper meaning. Almost overnight, Christmas Eve became one of those "silent nights" to ponder the miracle of Jesus.

The sanctuary was dark but oh so warm. Up and down each pew, a candle was passed to light the one we held in our hands. When mine was lit, I held it tightly, staring into the flame. I felt as though I were holding something holy. When I leaned on the kneelers to pray, I tried to make my prayer last as long as the little candle, as though that would be proof of my heart's desire that this be an important night. I wanted Jesus to know how special I thought he was.

On this side of eternity, Christmas is still a promise. Yes, the Savior has come, and with him peace on earth, but the story is not finished. Yes, there is peace in our hearts, but we long for peace in our world.

And pray I did, long and earnestly. But as I sat back into the pew, I expected something else to happen. Something to fill that strange longing inside me.

It's a longing that believers across the centuries have had in their hearts.

God announced his intentions about the Messiah when he made a promise to Abraham. And what did Abraham do? Romans 4:3 tells us that he believed God. That's all he needed to do. The rest was credited to him as righteousness.

But I wonder how Abraham felt two weeks later. Or months later. How did his children feel many years later? And what about his descendants, thousands of years later? How long did these people wait before they finally stopped believing?

The fact is, many did stop believing. They had no faith. They didn't reckon that God was a promise keeper. As a result, they had no righteousness to their credit.

But others continued to believe. They dreamed of the day, they hoped for the future, they put their confidence in the promise of God. These, no doubt, were the ones who recognized Christmas when it happened. These were the ones who knew Jesus. These were the ones who waited for the promise. Zechariah, in Luke 1, said, "Praise be to the Lord, the God of Israel, because he has come . . . (as he said through his holy prophets of long ago) . . . to remember his holy covenant, the oath he swore to our father Abraham" (Luke 1:68, 70, 72–73). Zechariah, and many like him, didn't stop believing. And their faith was credited to them as righteousness.

On this side of eternity, Christmas is still a promise. Yes, the Savior has come, and with him peace on earth, but the story is not finished. Yes, there is peace in our hearts, but we long for peace in our world.

Every Christmas is still a "turning of the page" until Jesus returns. Every December 25 marks another year that draws us closer to the fulfillment of the ages, that draws us closer to . . . home.

When we realize that Jesus is the answer to our deepest longing, even Christmas longings, each Advent brings us closer to his glorious return to earth. When we see him as he is, King of kings and Lord of lords, that will be "Christmas" indeed!

Talk about giving Christmas gifts! Just think of this abundance . . .

You do not lack any spiritual gift as you eagerly wait for our Lord Jesus Christ to be revealed. (1 Cor. 1:7)

And carols? You're about to hear singing like you've never heard before. Listen . . .

Then I heard something like the voice of a great multitude and like the sound of many waters and like the sound of mighty peals of thunder, saying, "Hallelujah! For the Lord our God, the Almighty, reigns." (Rev. 19:6, NASB)

Christmas choirs? Never was there a choir like the one about to be assembled . . .

> They held harps given them by God and sang . . . the song of the Lamb: "Great and marvelous are your deeds, Lord God Almighty. Just and true are your ways, King of the ages." (Rev. 15:2–3)

True, Main Street in your town may be beautifully decorated for the season, but picture this . . .

> The twelve gates [of the city] were twelve pearls, each gate made of a single pearl. The great street of the city was of pure gold, like transparent glass. (Rev. 21:21)

Oh, and yes, we love the glow of candles on a cold winter's night and the twinkling of Christmas lights in the dark, but can you imagine this?

> There will be no more night. They will not need the light of a lamp or the light of the sun, for the Lord God will give them light. And they will reign for ever and ever. (Rev. 22:5)

Heaven is about to happen. The celebration is about to burst on the scene. We stand tiptoe at the edge of eternity, ready to step into the new heaven and the new earth. And I can hardly wait.

I can't wait to sing "O Come, All Ye Faithful" as I gather with my friends and family to worship the Lord in heaven. I can't wait to give him the gift of my refined faith, the "riches of his glorious inheritance in the saints" (Eph. 1:18). On bended knee, alongside kings and shepherds, together we will praise him and sing "Glory to God in the highest" (Luke 2:14)! And for eternity we will follow the one who is "the bright Morning Star" (Rev. 22:16).

Christmas is an invitation to a celebration yet to happen. If you've got a Christmas longing, you're about to be satisfied, too. Just hold on and say with me . . . Maranatha! Come Lord!

Excerpted from *A Christmas Longing* by Joni Eareckson Tada. Copyright © 1990, 1996 by Joni Eareckson Tada. Used by permission of WaterBrook Multnomah Publishing Group, a division of Random House, Inc.

Unless otherwise indicated, Scripture quotations are from the New International Version.

Notes

Chapter 2: Tabernacled among Us

1. Attributed to John Francis Wade, "O Come, All Ye Faithful," *Trinity Hymnal* (Philadelphia: Great Commission Publications, 1961), 208.

2. John Donne, "Christmas Day, 1626," in *Sermons of John Donne,* ed. Evelyn M. Simpson and George R. Potter (Berkeley: University of California Press, 1962), 7:279.

Chapter 5: The Gifts of Christmas

1. C. S. Lewis, *The Four Loves* (New York: Harcourt Trade Publishers, 2003), 121.

2. Dorothy L. Sayers, *Christian Letters to a Post-Christian World* (Grand Rapids, MI: Eerdmans, 1969), 14.

Chapter 13: Wrapped in Humility

1. Edward Caswall, "See, Amid the Winter's Snow," 1851.

Chapter 14: Shepherd Status

1. Joachim Jeremias, "The Shepherd in Later Judaism," in *Theological Dictionary of the New Testament,* ed. Gerhard Friedrich and Geoffrey W. Bromiley (Grand Rapids, MI: Eerdmans, 1968), 6:489.

2. Ibid.

3. Ibid.

Chapter 16: Good News of Great Joy

1. Richard Sibbes, *Works of Richard Sibbes* (Carlisle, PA: Banner of Truth, 1981), 5:298f.

Chapter 21: Those to Whom Christ Comes

1. James Hastings, ed., *The Speaker's Bible*, vol. 9 (Grand Rapids, MI: Baker, 1971), 163. Hastings attributes this line to Richard Crashaw.

Also Available
from Nancy Guthrie

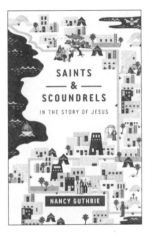

Seeing Jesus in the Old Testament Series

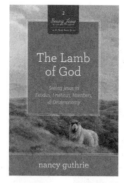

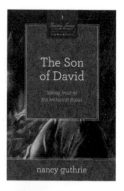

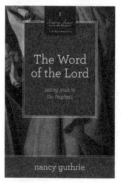

In these 10-week studies, Nancy Guthrie guides small groups to see the overarching theme of the work of Christ found in the Old Testament.

For more information, visit **crossway.org**.